LITERARY CONTEXTS

Victorian Literature

Literary Contexts recognises that literature is always rooted in its social milieu and that we need to study literary cultures in all their complexity and connections. It offers the thrill of locating a text within its context and seeing a context reflected in a literary/cultural text.

Each of the books in the series offers students of English and other literatures concise, informative insights into the history of ideas embodied in literary texts, authors and movements. Organised around themes and ideas with extensive examples from literary and cultural texts, the books enable students to understand how the "literary" takes shape in an intellectual milieu and discover manifestations of abstract ideas in literary texts. Written by scholar-teachers who have taught and researched literature for several years, each volume in the series is a stand-alone reference book for students and teachers alike.

Series editor

Pramod K. Nayar teaches at the Department of English, University of Hyderabad. His most recent books include *The Indian Graphic Novel: Nation, History and Critique* (2016), *The Transnational in English Literature: Shakespeare to the Modern* (2015), *Citizenship and Identity in the Age of Surveillance* (2015) and *The Postcolonial Studies Dictionary* (2015). His forthcoming work include *Human Rights and Literature* and *The Extreme in Contemporary Culture: States of Vulnerability.*

Also in the series

Shakespeare
American Literature
Modern English Literature, 1890–1960
Postcolonial Literatures
Postmodern Literatures
Eighteenth-century English Literature

Literary Contexts

Victorian Literature

Pradipta Borgohain

Series Editor
Pramod K. Nayar

Orient BlackSwan

VICTORIAN LITERATURE

ORIENT BLACKSWAN PRIVATE LIMITED

Registered Office
3-6-752 Himayatnagar, Hyderabad 500 029, Telangana, India
e-mail: centraloffice@orientblackswan.com

Other Offices
Bengaluru, Bhopal, Chennai, Guwahati, Hyderabad, Jaipur, Kolkata, Lucknow, Mumbai, New Delhi, Noida, Patna, Vijayawada

First published 2017

ISBN 978 93 86296 97 9

024963
17012017

Typeset in Adobe Caslon Pro 11.5/14.3 *by*
OSDATA, Hyderabad

Printed and bound at
Graphica Printers & Binders, Hyderabad 500 013

Published by
Orient Blackswan Private Limited
3-6-752 Himayatnagar, Hyderabad 500 029, Telangana, India
e-mail: info@orientblackswan.com

CONTENTS

Series Editor's Preface

The idea that the literature of every age is rooted in its social milieu is a truism. Mapping the contours of this milieu often requires, for the student, to read through several specialised texts. Titles in *Literary Contexts*, by bringing together the key contexts – both general and specialised – into one volume, offer the student of English and other literatures short, prescient and informative studies that provide the history of ideas embodied in literary texts, authors and movements.

Intellectual history or the history of ideas has always been intertwined with the cultural practices and shifts within them in every age. Therefore titles in the series track the intellectual history of every age through social and historical contexts, whether these were contexts of imperial voyages, "Westward expansion", the Reformation of the Church, great scientific discoveries or nationalist movements. Considerable attention is paid to the contexts of class, literacy, gender relations, the state and its functions in every age.

The series' titles demonstrate how certain dominant ideas in any age operated. To this end, every title in the series draws upon and cites numerous examples from literary texts. This enables the student to get a sense of the literary themes' origins in the intellectual milieu, and discover manifestations of abstract ideas, such as "exceptionalism", "hybrid and displaced identity" or "division of powers of Church and State", in literary texts.

The authors do not seek to establish a direct correspondence between the literary text and the dominant idea of the age, but they offer the student a sense of the dense exchanges between the idea and the literary text. Each title maps ideas across cultural texts – popular forms, high culture, and scientific and philosophical texts – so that it demonstrates how ideas are mobile and cut across genres and domains. The titles in the series also document the conflicts and tensions in every age so that the student is made aware of the complicated nature of both, the history of ideas and the literary expressions of the same, and is alerted to the messy nature of cultural history of any age, in any nation.

Written by scholar-teachers who have taught and researched literature for several years, *Literary Contexts* is student-friendly, being both jargon-free and incisive.

Pramod K. Nayar

Introduction

Queen Victoria, the long-reigning monarch of Great Britain, lent her name to a period of history marked by a series of exciting and transformational events. While officially the Victorian era runs from 1837, the year of her ascent to the throne of England, to 1901, the year of her death, periodisations are never exact, and it can be argued that many developments which are identified as typically Victorian were visible before her coronation, just as tendencies characteristic of the subsequent "modern" age were well under way before her death. Nevertheless, the sheer length of the Victorian period imposes its own uniformity, and some of its distinguishing features are unarguable. Some of these features which also became popular themes for literary artists are: a belief in progress (and sometimes, even a *need* to believe in progress), moral earnestness and didacticism, work-ethics, family values, a more coherent, deliberate, and aggressive kind of imperialism, class-consciousness or snobbery, class-conflict, religious anguish and soul-searching, stir for women's rights, and "scientific" racism. This list is by no means exhaustive.

While human history has never known a condition of stasis, the Victorian period was a time of change like no other that had gone before. Most of the groundbreaking changes took place in the spheres which have been identified as important contexts for the study of literature in this book: religion, science, industrialism and class, empire, women's rights, and education. Such an ordering may exclude a few interesting aspects of Victorian culture and society such as crime, health and sanitation. However, I am looking at only those aspects which have most fascinated the creative mind and have later been absorbed into the literary history of the period because of the way they have been absorbed into literary writings, from a variety of perspectives. The choice of contexts here may be inclusive enough to present a coherent portrait of a society passing through a particularly interesting and intriguing period of history. The Industrial Revolution and the development of science at the time were remarkable forces of change, while religion was largely resistant to change and had a stake in the perpetuation of the status quo. But all three willy-nilly participate in the drama of change that was sweeping over Great Britain.

While the structure or ordering of the book – with science, religion and other subjects treated in separate chapters – is convenient and facilitates the reader's comprehension, it helps to remember that the issues discussed are closely interlinked and connected. This is a point I get back to repeatedly in the book. Some of the connections and interrelations are only too obvious. Science with its many inventions contributes to the Industrial Revolution just as the Industrial Revolution itself helps science to steam ahead. A more negative example of causal connection is the turmoil and despair generated in the realm of religion by science, in particular Darwinian evolutionary science. Sometimes the interrelations are comparatively more subtle, and it is these subtle and not so palpable connections that historians and literary artists unmask. To give an example: on the face of it, there is no clear-cut link between the many revolutionary and turbulent events of the century and the issue of women's rights. Many of these events were on a wide and grand scale: in the beginning of the nineteenth century Napoleon was strutting on the European stage and flaunting his powers, and the middle of the century was shaken by the democratic revolutions which had swept through the Continent while in England the Chartists were creating a storm. The movement for women's rights, on the other hand, was seemingly a tamer, quieter affair. Most women were confined to their homes, and many believed themselves to be content with their domestic roles. However, it is possible to detect even in small gestures the seeds of future upheavals and the implications of something larger. Historian F. M. L. Thompson (whose exact words I will quote in their proper context) draws a connection between the unquiet times and looming feminine rebellion. The literary critic Robert Polhemus also reads a lot into a seemingly trivial gesture made by Becky Sharp who throws away Dr Johnson's dictionary at the beginning of the semi-historical novel *Vanity Fair:* "It is a revolutionary act, desecrating decorum and the authority of the past . . . Dr Johnson is gone; Napoleon rules" (Polhemus 131).

Many other such fascinating connections between worlds seemingly poles apart from one another can be detected, and one of the purposes of this book is to encourage students to make such connections. Another thing to note is that whether crossing over from one world to another, or tracing various lines of continuities and causalities, it is also important to not ignore paradoxes and contradictions which break up smooth, linear progressions. In an age as vast and complex as the Victorian, it is particularly important to problematise issues rather than come up with the neatest and most convenient summary or explanation. In all the chapters, dealing with various aspects of Victorian life, a certain chronology is inevitable. But if we join chronology with progress (which many Victorians wanted to), problems arise. The Industrial Revolution, which ushered in great comfort and prosperity for many people, and established Great Britain as the dominant power on the global stage, also brought in untold misery for many. In fact, it created newer forms of misery, and created populaces seemingly defined by their distressful living conditions. Science, a force for progress without parallel and competition, unearthed a new interest in primitivism and also exposed many regressive tendencies of human existence. The condition of women improved in different ways, but as works such as *The Odd Women* reveal, also deteriorated in some other ways. The old family-structures had crumbled, and a more competitive way of life, going by the name of Social Darwinism, was taking over, making life difficult for many. The very notion of progress was controversial. Progress essentially translated into material progress, and there was clamorous criticism by many writers, thinkers, and theologians of the period of the ever-expanding materialism of the times. It helps a student to keep in mind many of these issues while looking at various contexts for the production and consumption of literary texts.

The Victorian age was genuinely progressive, as various Reform Acts, each building on the achievements and shortcomings of the previous one, attest. Many Victorians, including scientists, realised that the past is also an ever-present reality, that progress itself and our understanding of the present and anticipations of the future are dependent on paying due respect to the past. A dynamic or "progressive" tracking of interrelated developments is essential as human civilisation does not rest at any milepost but keeps going forward unceasingly. This is a lesson that is common to historians, scientists, and literary artists alike, and writers from these fields, Carlyle and Macaulay, Eliot and Hardy, and the great Darwin himself, paid due attention to the role of the past.

In the Victorian age Great Britain's concerns took on a panoramic, world-wide aura with imperialism consolidating itself in many parts of the globe. The writers also found a wide array of subject matters to deal with, with imperial themes trickling in at unsuspected moments. The home situation also became more crowded and complex, with the expansions of cities due to large-scale migrations from the green countryside to the gray urbanscapes, creating a host of new classes. The "coming out" of women and the assertiveness of religiously marginalised groups such as the Dissenters contributed their own complexity. While many old traditions, dogmas and pieties started fading in the face of new developments, a modern note started creeping into the poetry of writers such as Tennyson, Arnold, Hopkins and Meredith. As for the novelists, in the heyday of the Victorian novel they responded to a more populous and fragmented world by writing multi-plot novels which tried to accommodate different interlocking plot-lines reflecting the stories of different classes and professions. However, the changing dynamics of readership and publishing including newer uses of leisure time meant that novelists would switch over to more compact forms of writing as the century wound to a close.

In this book, I have tried to note some of the unique trends of Victorian society which have complicated and stimulated literary response, keeping facts and figures to a minimum. Students can do more work unearthing basic relevant information, depending on where their requirements lie. I have also used only a very limited numbers of writers as exemplars, as the point of certain observations and interpretations may become blurred if the works of too many writers are taken into consideration. Also, the focus is mainly on the novelists. One reason for this is that the novel was the dominant form in the Victorian period. Additionally, novels with their broader canvases and their greater inclusivity can better highlight many contextual aspects – religious, social or commercial – that it is the business of a book of this nature to draw attention to. Occasional literary interpretation of writers and their texts is inevitable. Such interpretations are, however, offered not so much to assess and assert the merit of the author, but to aid in the process of highlighting important cultural trends and currents of thought. After all, very often it is literary texts that most memorably capture the essence of a moment and preserve it for future generations.

Works Cited

Polhemus, Robert. *Comic Faith: The Great Tradition from Austen to Joyce.* Chicago: U of Chicago P, 1980. Print.

ONE

The Crisis in Religion

It is a widely acknowledged fact that in nineteenth-century England, religion was in a state of crisis. However, it is also true that there were revivals and rallies. The growth of a revivalist phenomenon such as the Oxford Movement captured the imagination of many and seemed to give a new direction and boost to Christianity. But on the whole, religion was in retreat and would never quite recover its earlier authority.

There were many reasons for this state of affairs. "Enemies" of Christianity were many. From the broadest of perspectives one would be right to notice a general drift towards a lifestyle no longer tethered to religious conformity or submission to ecclesiastical discipline. Yet, one would also rightly notice that a great deal of the crisis was engendered, not from the outside by "secularizing" forces, but from within. The Oxford Movement mentioned above is an instance of intra-religious strife that actually turned into full-blown separation or schism, dealing a body blow to the official Church of England.

While the complex moments of internecine warfare deserve careful and sustained scrutiny, one may as well begin with the simplest of everyday practices while broaching the subject of religious crisis: the fact that church attendance was on the decline. An official census of religious attendance was held on 30 March 1851. The result showed that about seven million people out of about eighteen million inhabitants of England and Wales attended church services. Beginning his chapter on religion with this census and giving these figures, Philip Davis in *The Victorians* goes on to say: "It was a shock. Only half the nation was attending religious services; only a quarter was attending the services of the established national Church" (99). The actual attendance figures may also obscure a reality that would be a rude check on the optimism of the genuinely devout – that one often attended merely as social gesture, so as not to be left out of the collective experience and belongingness. Such is the attitude, for instance, of the fairly devout Phillip (he actually dies with God's name on his lips) in the novel *Sylvia's Lovers* (1863): "He believed that he went because he thought it right to attend public worship in the parish church whenever it was offered up; but it may be questioned of him, as of many others, how far he would have been as regular in attendance in a place where he was not known" (358; Ch. XXXI).

However, while all this may be regarded as telling evidence of the decline of the Church, and also a sign of a future where church-going and other gestures of conformity and piety would recede in the face of "competition" from other social habits such as sports and get-togethers in clubs, it is still well to be cautious and not jump to easy and simple generalisations. On the one hand, erosion of the Church's authority was undeniable. On the other hand (and at certain other levels) however, religion continued to be a force to contend with. Sermons and religious literature continued to be extremely popular. Singing of church hymns in public places often made people bond together, and writers also emulated such hymns while writing poetry. Also, while sections of the general public may have become apathetic towards the forms and ceremonies of Christianity, large sections of the intelligentsia, the writing community and academics continued to fervently debate about questions of religion, keeping it in the forefront of public notice.

Before going any further, however, it would be proper to give a sense of the positions and relative strengths and weaknesses of the different denominations that dotted the face of Victorian Christianity. The Church of England was the Protestant Anglican Church since the seventeenth century, holding a middle-ground between Roman Catholics on one side and the Puritans on the other. The Puritans would pass on their inheritance to the Evangelicals, and in this avatar become more mainstream. The Roman Catholics, on the other hand, after facing some persecution and denial of rights during parts of the seventeenth and eighteenth centuries, would recover some lost ground in the reformist nineteenth century. The social scene in respect of religious affiliations would get crowded and complicated by the arrival and consolidation of numerous dissenting sects such as the Quakers, the Independents and the Baptists. The curious groundbreaking practices of these energetic and energising dissenting sects played a significant role in the readjustment of social positions as well as in the creation or activation of newer forms of challenges to ecclesiastical and even political authority. In the words of E. F. Biagini,

> Radical liberty was indeed rooted in the history, practice, and ideology of Protestant Nonconformity. Congregationalists, Baptists, Quakers, Unitarians, Free Presbyterians (all forming the so-called Old Dissent), and the Methodists (New Dissent) provided the backbone of radical and labour movements in Victorian and Edwardian Britain. (Biagini 102–03)

The affairs of all these religions created reverberations across society, and in particular manifestations and intense forms engaged the attention of writers. The writers treating religious subjects expressed themselves in short or lengthy prose works including memoirs and letters, as well as in poems, and of course in, novels – the dominant literary form of the century.

To get one's bearing in the religious terrain of nineteenth-century England, apart from acquainting oneself with the destinies of marginal groups such as the Dissenters and the Roman Catholics, it is also important to have a sense of the conflict or opposition that raged in the heart of the Protestant, official church – the one between the High Church, Low Church, and the Broad Church. This conflict is treated with great comic verve and gusto by Anthony Trollope in the high-spirited comedy of *Barchester Towers* (1857), where the adherents of the High and Low Church parties don armour and sail into a non-holds-barred battle to the finish, fighting for power and supremacy in the serene English countryside of the imaginary land of Barset. This work, as well as its predecessor *The Warden* (1854), wonderfully capture the sheer ludicrousness of religious strife that gets diverted from the serious or doctrinal aspects of religious conduct into mundane matters of pelf and power. The very chapter headings such as "Who Shall be Cock of the Walk?" in *Barchester Towers* debunk the positions of the antagonists. However, there are several other instances of the Victorian creative mind finding out and exposing the greed and hypocrisy of the clergy.

In the more serious work *Shirley* (1849), preoccupied with industrial conflict on the one hand and the crisis of identity for women on the other, Charlotte Bronte spares a sardonic thought for the mindless wrangling and the petty vanities of the men in cloth, beginning her novel with the expression "an abundant shower of curates" (1; Ch 1). In that work, apart from the nominal hero and heroine figures (those who figure in the love plots which are important for providing the narrative with conventionally satisfactory closures), many of the important characters are men with various religious designations to their names. Few of them emerge with any credit after the dust settles down at the end.

However, to deal with certain "real" issues: the High Church was the most dominant and numerically the largest faction within the Church throughout the century. They were the conservatives, in keeping with their dominant status, adhering to tradition and ceremony. While they anathemise the Catholics and the Dissenters almost in equal measure while staying within the establishment, their essential habits and beliefs ally them more with the Roman Catholics than with others within the established church. The potential for certain sections of the official clergy toppling over into "the cesspool of Rome" (an expression used by the narrator in *Barchester Towers*) (111; Vol. 1, Ch. 14), was of course an ever-present "danger," – one reason for the suspicion with which Roman Catholics were held in England and the restrictions that were imposed on them.

The Roman Catholics became associated with the love of ease, idleness, pomp and the good things of life. At their worst, some of them were seen as corrupt and decadent. More positively, the High Church could be more tolerant towards others, and not prone to harrying others with a rhetoric of sin and damnation or try and persuade everyone about the necessity of a life of austerity and incessant work like the Low Church people were apt to do. ("Low Church" is an eighteenth-century designation separating them from the authority-bound High Church, and it was in the nineteenth century that it became synonymous with the Evangelists while the liberal traditions of the Low Church found expression and new life in the Broad Church – exclusively a nineteenth-century formation). Trollope pokes fun at clergymen of all hues and dispositions. Nevertheless, the scenario that emerges in *Barchester Towers* is that it is the High Church party led by Archdeacon Grantley that comes across as being more humane and less oppressive than the aggressively power-seeking and persecuting Low Church led by Bishop Proudie, his chaplain Slope, and his wife. It is true that the Low Church *seems* more tolerant, but that is really a matter of policy, part of the power game that these particular partisans of the Low Church incessantly play.

The leaning towards a life of enjoyment at the cost of one's essential religious (and by extension, social) duties, was not confined only to the party that could be identified as the High

Church. There was a feeling among many concerned with the health of the Christian community that if the slide into indifference or worse was allowed to go unchecked, a state of anarchy might prevail, and there would be the reign of the devil. While criticism was often levelled against clergymen regarding the dereliction of their duties, the common enemy of different religious factions was secularisation or godlessness. While the Evangelicals were the most fierce and relentless pursuers of secular or irreverent tendencies, one of the most famous religious movements of Victorian England, namely the Tractarian or Oxford movement led by the likes of John Newman, Hurrell Froude , Edward Pusey and John Keble, also had as its basis a renewed defence of the faith. This was instigated by the perceived threat of secularisation (as liberal voices seemed to be on the ascendant) as well as of laxity of the clergy. The flirtation with what was called the Higher Criticism – whereby the actual historical circumstances of the Holy Scriptures were investigated and the humanity rather than divinity of Christ was explored – caused chagrin among the orthodox that were for blind faith in Revelation. There were times when such bitter enemies as the Evangelicals and the Tractarians actually agreed with one another.

The Tractarians opposed Parliament's intervention in spiritual or clerical matters. Keble's famous sermon called "National Apostasy", delivered in St Mary's Church in 1833, is regarded as the inaugural moment of the Oxford Movement. In this he lamented the rule of the "Earthly King" which was being heralded by various reforms, the hostility of the nation to the Holy Church, and a general decay of faith. The specific provocation was the Church Temporalities (Ireland) Act 1833 which was part of the reformist drive under way in Victorian England. This piece of legislation tried to reorganise religious administration by suppressing ten bishoprics in Ireland and merging the corresponding dioceses. This act could be seen as an encroachment into the rights and privileges of the Church in a way which could hold damaging implications for the future.

Certain tracts published between 1833 and 1841 and numbering about 90, were written by the divines mentioned above and a few others, and together were known as *Tracts for the Times.* It is from these that the Oxford movement derived its secondary name. The tracts addressed matters pertaining to the gospel, rituals, and the apostolic succession. In general, the Tractarians were concerned to elevate faith over reason or any other liberal and secular notion, and also to champion the idea of an undivided universal Catholic Church. The poetry and prose of these divines is often steeped in mysticism, as they believed that there were hidden spiritual realties underneath or behind the common light of day. Only an inner light or conviction could guide one towards these, and not reason or practical common sense. They were also greatly against the idea of Dissent which was getting such a grip on the minds of the people, as in their view the Dissenting spirit allowed an individual choice when it came to religious matters. In their tracts and sermons as well as in their poems and other forms of writing they opposed such concessions to the spirit of individualism and defended authority and tradition.

John Henry Newman who would become the face of the Oxford Movement more than anybody else, primarily because of his great skills of writing, displayed in works such as the autobiography *Apologia Pro Vita Sua, The Idea of a University,* and poems such as "Lead Kindly Light," dealt deeply with matters of the soul in his sermons and longer works, helping to dissever the association of the High Church from material concerns of preferments, livings, sinecures, and the like. However, the fact remains that finally Newman broke ranks with even the High Church in England and went over to the bosom of the Mother Church in 1845, namely Roman Catholicism. This was certainly a setback for the Tractarians as they were trying to find a middle path between the Church of Rome and sections of the Church of England who seemed to be compromising with the secularists and the liberals.

The High Church and the Low Church settling on two extremes of the Protestant Church, and in different ways being intolerant, severe and judgemental while trying to earn for Christianity a more dominant role and status, it was left to numerically the least among these "parties," that is the Broad Church, to steer a middle way. It was they, more than any other religious sect or denomination, who addressed "that central question of the nineteenth century: how to reconcile the existence of an all-loving, all-powerful God with the concept of eternal punishment" (Wolff 307).The proponents of the Broad Church ideology pleaded directly or obliquely for a more humane, compassionate and adaptive and accommodative attitude towards society on the part of religion. As the term itself implies, they were for a broader philosophy or way of life, an inclusiveness that would build up a harmonious national consensus in matters religious or spiritual. Liberals in political outlook (in contrast with the High Church who were Tories for the most part), they also were willing to embrace new scientific insights. One of the most well-known proponents of this ideology was Thomas Arnold, the father of Mathew Arnold, who was arguably the most famous educationist of the nineteenth century. Among writers of the period, Charles Kingsley and Thomas Hughes and even Charles Dickens can be counted as proponents or supporters of the Broad Church philosophy. Although never the largest of the factions, the influence of the Broad Church grew as the century progressed while that of the Low Church or the Evangelicals declined to some extent.

There is much more to be said about the history of the fortunes of these parties as well as the implications of their codes, credos and working practices. We will also look at the way many well-known writers responded to the stances of the players in the religious terrain of Victorian England. However, it is time now to turn to some of the basic issues of religion that preoccupied the larger life of the nation, as well as some of the general reasons why Christianity declined with the progress of the century, or was forced to reach compromises with certain forces of modernity or secularity.

The fact was that despite the undeniable erosion of clerical authority, religion was a potent and indeed popular subject. It would not be an exaggeration to say that there was a national obsession with religion. In the words of John Maynard,

> No subject occupied the Victorians, certainly not identity politics, or sexuality, or the empire, or even politics, as much – in the privacy of their meditations and in the public outpouring of their endless works, sermons, tracts, confessions, spiritual autobiographies, interpretations and re-interpretations of every aspect of the Bible and the Church fathers – as religion. (192)

In particular, the issues of sin and damnation, God's judgement, the reality of heaven and hell, and the links between present life and the afterlife or the hereafter haunted men and women and prompted them to engage in conversations, debates and polemics. Many of these issues would also be taken up by the novelists and poets and given different spins and interpretations, memorialising them for future generations in a way that could not be done by academics and divines.

Heaven and hell had an almost Miltonic reality for many people, in a way that is perhaps not imaginable in today's world. To disbelieve in heaven and hell would be regarded as blasphemous for Victorians, whatever branch of the ecclesiastical establishment he might be affiliated to, although dissenting views or beliefs were no longer met with the kind of punishment that was reserved for heretics and freethinkers in previous ages. But among the believers, there were different shades of opinions regarding the shape of heaven and hell. For many, heaven was not so much a concretely imaginable place, the celestial city with a specific layout and radiant visibility, but a somewhat vague notion of a time to be spent in eternal comfort after an earthly life spent in virtuous toil. It could also be something that one looked forward perhaps in a spirit of wish-fulfilment after the often harsh and dreary experience of this life. As Michael Wheeler points out, heaven could be "a socially useful refuge from appalling social conditions" (121). Creative writers resorted to the imagery of light to hint at the kind of emotional space that heaven might provide. And then there was a feeling among some, including the great John Henry Newman, that heaven was right here although perhaps not quite visible to the eye.

Hell, a concept intertwined with the notion of heaven, was perhaps a more controversial subject. The Victorian Age was a period when liberal thinking on many matters received a lot of encouragement from many quarters and from different social developments, and in the light of this, it was often not desirable or possible to persist with the medieval notions of eternal punishment for the ungodly. Yet, there was no dearth of people to paint vivid, terrifying pictures of hell. For instance, Michael Heller gives the example of Father Furnell, author of a penny booklet called *The Sight of Hell* (1861) who conjured frightening visions of hell for children, so that they would be properly chastened. He puts these words into the mouth of Christ in his booklet: "It was a mercy that the punishment of Hell was made everlasting. If so many broke my law, knowing that the punishment would be everlasting, how would it have been, if the punishment had not been everlasting?" (Wheeler 180). Phyllis Bentley, a modern biographer of the Brontës, gives the example of Reverend Carus Wilson, who was made notorious as the headmaster Brocklehurst by Charlotte Bronte in *Jane Eyre*: "anyone who has read one of his little *Children's friend* magazines or his stories for children, cannot but agree with a shudder that his conception of the right kind of tuition for children was totally and most horribly wrong." Children pray for death or when naughty, are struck by death and go to hell. Another child is informed that children are whipped so that their souls are saved (Bentley 25–26). However, perhaps more than these crusaders for assertion of a medieval hell-view, the resistance to notions of hellfire and damnation on the part of those who wanted to usher in a kinder, gentler Christianity was the more remarkable. Indeed, Michael Wheeler points out that "by 1890 the idea of endless physical punishment had been discredited in the more liberal Protestant traditions, and even moderated in English Roman Catholic circles" (178). It was due to the efforts of Broad Church theologians such as F. D. Maurice and his disciple F. W. Farrar – author of the appropriately titled *Eternal Hope* – that the harsher aspects of Christianity in the areas of God's judgment and the reality of hell were mitigated along the course of the century.

Such thinkers and writers wished to stress God's mercy rather than His wrath. They often resorted to well-thought-out argumentation to plead for a greater belief in the reality of a caring God and to discredit the stance of doomsayers who emphasised the fallen state of humankind. Someone like Farrar tried to combat the bleak Calvinist (after John Calvin, a Swiss theologian born in France) view that except for a handful of the "elect," that is a chosen few, all bore the mark of original sin and therefore were doomed due to no fault of theirs.

Broad Church liberals tried to win for religion a more acceptable profile while Roman Catholics, some High Church adherents and some Protestants like the Evangelicals and the Calvinists often chose to stress the harsher aspects of Christianity such as irreversible doom for most of humanity and the unavoidable reality of suffering for the sinning in hell. However, although the attitude of clergymen became more tolerant and forgiving as the century progressed, religion itself lost its aura and powers to console. Clergymen indulged in doctrinal debates, while many ordinary Victorians retreated into an evasive sentimentality to avoid the terrors of life. Science made it increasingly difficult to come up with religious solutions and interpretations – whether optimistic and reassuring or dark and chastening. While the revelations of science belong to another chapter, it needs to be pointed out that many Victorians constructed private edifices and comfort zones often in the face of contrary scientific evidence. Thus Tennyson, after confronting the annihilating evidence of geological sciences, reaches a kind of compromise by thinking of some kind reunion with his beloved Hallam in heaven. This wish-fulfilment is in line with what Wheeler calls heavens actually turning into a middle-class suburb: "Perhaps the most characteristic Victorian ideas of heaven are of a place in which family reunions and 'the recognition of friends' are to be achieved after death . . . such heavens are often more like a middle-class suburb in the sky than the city of God . . ." (120–21).

Life all round often being not exactly ideal, with poverty or its opposite rank materialism pressing in upon the consciousnesses and consciences of sensitive people, literary artists often thought about the rewards of afterlife. The notorious Victorian sentimentality often underlay such depictions. Clergymen tactically dangled the promises of afterlife before the poor and the working-classes in order to neutralise radical aspirations of doing something about the flawed conditions of this life. The afterlife hinted at by creative writers was a little different. Theirs was an imaginative endeavour, sentimental and emotional in nature, a private vision that probably reflected a collective emotional thirst for reassurance. Ignoring in some ways the evidences given by science and material progress, or on the other hand, the dogmas of the Church, writers such as Charles Dickens often posited a vision of transcendence that took one beyond the grim and irreparable mortal human world. At such moments there is an abrupt descent (although the writer would see it as an ascent) from the concrete and penetrative portrayal of real life to puerile sentimentality. In *The Old Curiosity Shop* (1840–41), Little Nell dreams that a little student who dies of illness has mingled with angels: "Her dreams were of the little scholar: not coffined and covered up, but mingled with angels, and smiling happily" (198; Ch. 26). When Nell herself dies, Dickens succumbs to the temptation of becoming teary and preachy and exploiting the full sentimental potential of the scene: "When Death strikes down the innocent and young, for every fragile form from which he lets the panting spirit free, a hundred virtues rise, in shapes of mercy, charity and love, to walk the world and bless it" (543; Ch.72).

In his later novels, however, Dickens is a little more successful in pitting a glimmer of future religious fulfilment against secular injustice or oppression. In *Great Expectations* (1861) such an expression of faith is no mere sentimental indulgence, but a symbolic rendering of divine justice which is memorable and effective. In *Hard Times* (1854) the long-suffering Stephen departs from this world after not receiving any rewards for his patience and his virtuous conduct. However, in the loving figure of the biblically named Rachael, he has some solace that has a flavour of the divine about it: "As the shining stars were to the heavy candle ... so was Rachael ..." (119; Bk 1, Ch. XIII). At the moment of his death, there is a symbolic hint that he may be redeemed in the afterlife, with the same starlight imagery hanging over him in his final moment.

In *Great Expectations* we see the essentially good Magwitch brought to book and facing trial due to a system of administering justice that takes no note of the factors that turned him into a criminal. Human justice is flawed and inadequate to reward and punish according to the true merit of the case, but there is a possibility of redemption in eternity: "the sun was striking in at the great windows of the court, through the glittering drops of rain upon the glass, and it made a broad shaft of light between the two-and-thirty and the Judge, linking both together, and perhaps reminding some among the audience, how both were passing on, with absolute equality, to the greater Judgment that knoweth all things and cannot err" (390; Ch. 56). These moments are more successful or persuasive instances of Victorians finding in religion a consolation, and a way to endure stoically in this life of trials and tribulations in the light of future justice.

However, Dickens was not overtly a religious writer. While he lets the readers sample a transcendent and transfiguring hope by providing a few instances of a vision beyond this life, like many other Victorian novelists he actually subjected Victorian religion to acute criticism for many of its wrongdoings and failings. In the writings of Charles Dickens, as in the works of some of his contemporaries and successors, the custodians of religion and religious morality are seen as blighters of life, deniers of pleasure and happiness.

Writers such as Dickens and Charlotte Bronte are different in many ways, but they have both left behind strong indictments of Roman Catholicism in both their creative writings and in their letters and journalistic writings. This could be because they were proponents of a Romantic individualism in an age which was more inclined towards an acceptance of the rights of the community. Apart from being deemed guilty of upholding an enslaving traditionalism, Roman Catholics were believers in the unavoidability of inferno and the sinfulness of people. At their severest Catholics were no proponents of the happiness principle. However, to appreciate the reasons why writers often felt impelled to adopt an oppositional stance vis-à-vis organised religion or religion that took up a policing role, one needs to know a little more about Evangelism. Roman Catholicism was after all the faith of the minorities, and the Evangelicals played a much more central role in the moral life of the nation. Dickens himself, finding Protestantism in general synchronous with liberty and progress, seemed to abhor its extreme interpretation in the hands of some Evangelicals. People such as the Murdstones in *David Copperfield* and Mrs Clennam in *Little Dorrit* fall into this category.

Discussing the novels of Anthony Trollope, Christopher Herbert talks about the character of the Bishop's chaplain Slope as someone who stands for the wilful denial of pleasure (44). However, this is a comic work, and finally Slope is little more than a comic villain who brings some turbulence into the staid currents of life in Barset. It was not always possible to treat the Evangelicals or Low Church people in such a comic or light-hearted way. They were too earnest for that, and their reach too extensive.

The Evangelicals were the party of change. In *Barchester Towers* this aspect comes to the fore when the offensive Slope wounds the gentle High Churchman Harding by implicitly likening tradition-minded clergymen like him to "rubbish.": "And not only in Barchester, Mr. Harding, but in the world at large. It is not only in Barchester that a new man is carrying out new measures, and carting away the useless rubbish of past centuries" (99; Vol. 1, Ch. 12). This is the narrator's critical comment (reflecting the views of Harding) on the implications of Slope's words: "A man is sufficiently condemned if it can only be shown that either in politics or religion he does not belong to some new school established within the last score of years" (103).

However, the Evangelicals were indeed a force to reckon with in their genuine zeal to transform habits and manners such as riotous and drunken behaviour. They were often to be found on the deathbeds of people, asking for last-moment repentance or "conversion", which they believed was essential in order to be saved from eternal hellfire. They were invasive and irresistible, trying to connect with the common people and often succeeding in imposing their will and belief on the populace. However, while the Evangelicals were on a mission to change things, they were not out and out a party for progress. In fact, by the standards of the modern world, they might actually be regarded as regressive. Regarding themselves as the true heirs of Luther's Reformation, they wanted to bring about a kind of second reformation in the nineteenth century. But this reformation had a backward thrust in many ways. Often they came off not simply as anti-aesthetic but as anti-intellectual. In the words of Philip Davis, "Taking its name from its commitment to spreading the Evangel or the Gospel, Evangelicalism claimed to stand for a puritan renewal of the 'vital simplicities' of the old Reformation, purifying the faith of all ceremony and sacrament, the last formal traces of Roman Catholicism" (103).

Apart from its staunch opposition to Roman Catholicism (one reason why it became the "Low Church" in conflict with the "High Church" was because the latter showed Catholic tendencies) and in its privileging of emotion over reason, the Evangelicals also chose to become the stern guardians of social morality. It was this aspect of their religion, rather than their emotionalism or any particulars about church conduct and doctrinal matters, which earned them the fear and resentment of many people, a resentment that is reflected in the writings of Dickens, and later in the century – in the annihilating *The Way of All Flesh* by Samuel Butler. Philip Davis captures the persecuting moral sense of the Evangelicals in these words: "It emphasized the corruption of human nature, through the Fall into original sin: hence the inability of human beings, born into suffering and liable to damnation, to bring about their own salvation" (103). Davis goes on to remark: "Evangelicalism's God was a hard god" (104).

It is this hard God whose shadow falls on the protagonist of Dickens's late novel *Little Dorrit* (1857). The first glimpse of Arthur's childhood is mediated though the memory of strict Sunday observance:

> There was the dreary Sunday of his childhood, when he sat with his hands before him, scared out of his senses by a horrible tract which commenced to business with the poor child by asking him in its title, why he was going to Perdition? . . . There was the sleepy Sunday of his boyhood, when, like a military deserter, when he was marched to chapel by a piquet of teachers three times a day, morally handcuffed to another boy . . . .(24; Bk 1; Ch. 3)

It is the woman who he believes to be his mother, Mrs Clennam, who is responsible for this harsh regime under which he has to live. Apart from compelling Arthur to go through the dreary routine of church services on Sundays, she incarnates in general that spirit of the "hard God" mentioned by Davis:

> She then put on the spectacles and read certain passages aloud from a book – sternly, fiercely, wrathfully – praying that her enemies (she made them by her tone and manner expressly hers) might put to the edge of the sword, consumed by fire, smitten by plagues and leprosy, that their bones might be ground to the dust, and that they might be utterly exterminated. (29)

In Emily Bronte's *Wuthering Heights* (1847), the young Heathcliff and Catherine Earnshaw are compelled to go to church on Sunday like Arthur Clennam, but unlike Arthur, they rebel. The target of their rebellion is Catherine's despotic brother Hindley but also the judgemental Nonconformist Joseph, who like some others of his ilk, seems to go one better than the Evangelists in the matter of strict enforcement of the Sabbath. This is what Catherine's diary reveals about this particular "awful Sunday" of familial and religious oppression:

> I wish my father were back again. Hindley is a detestable substitute his conduct to Heathcliff is atrocious – H. And I are going to rebel – we took our initiatory step this evening . . . All day had been flooding with rain; we could not go to church, so Joseph must needs get up a congregation in the garret, and while Hindley and his wife basked downstairs before

> a comfortable fire – doing anything but reading their Bibles, I'll answer for it – Heathcliff, myself, and the unhappy plough-boy were commanded o take our Prayer-books and mount . . . (14; Ch. 3)

Sabbath observance was a big issue for the Evangelists – for anyone to work, travel or indulge in any activity pleasurable or otherwise on the day that God took rest was anathema to them. This aspect, treated seriously by Dickens and Brontë, comes in for mockery in *Barchester Towers.* Here the Sabbath is applied primarily in the suppression of pleasure, and not in the emulation of God's act of resting after six days of Creation:

> she [Mrs Proudie, the wife of the new bishop of Barset] is in her way a religious woman; and the form in which this religious tendency shows itself is by a strict observance of Sabbatarian rule. Dissipation and low dresses during the week are, under her control, atoned for by three services, an evening sermon read by herself, and a perfect abstinence from any cheering employment on the Sunday. (21; Vol. 1, Ch. 3)

In Victorian literature there is perhaps no more devastating indictment of the Evangelical code – and of the overtly and intrusively religious way of life in general – than Samuel Butler's *The Way of All Flesh* (1903). Butler started writing this work in the 1870s but it was finally published after his death, in the next century. It was a bombshell when it appeared in print, retrospectively shattering illusions of familial sanctity and harmony that were supposed to have been major props of Victorian life. However, the work's target is as much institutional religion as tyrannical parenthood. In fact, the tyranny and cruelty of parents is in large part owing to the ruthless Evangelical code that they have themselves suffered from, internalised and that they now use to smother their own children with.

The narrator says: "I think the Church Catechism has a good deal to do with the unhappy relations which commonly even now exist between parents and children. That work was written too exclusively from the parental point of view . . ." (41; Ch. 7). Parental tyranny and coerciveness is something handed down from generation to generation, and religion activates the worst kind of tyranny. George Pontifex blackmails his son Theobald into ordainment when the latter shows signs of dissidence and independence: "You shall not receive a single sixpence from me till you come to your senses" (46). A victim himself, Theobald becomes tyrannical in turn and makes his son Ernest a victim of religious persecution. This is the picture of the Pontifex household, run along the severest Evangelical lines:

> "I was there on a Sunday, and observed the rigour with which the young people were taught to observe the Sabbath; they might not cut out things, nor use their paint-box on a Sunday, and this they thought rather hard, because their cousins the John Pontifexes might do these things . . . One treat only was allowed them – on Sunday evenings they might choose their own hymns." (109; Ch. 22)

The sense of Christianity becoming a religion of fear at the hands of clergymen like Theobald is reinforced as we see him reading in a family setting those parts of the Old Testament (from *Numbers)* which emphasise the merciless rigour of God's justice:

> And while the children of Israel were in the wilderness they found a man that gathered sticks upon the Sabbath day. . .
>
> And the Lord said unto Moses, the man shall be surely put to death; all the congregation shall stone him with stones without the camp.
>
> And all the congregation brought him without the camp, and stoned him with stones, and he died; as the Lord commanded Moses. (112; Ch. 23)

While Butler is willing to acknowledge that "the spirit behind the Church is true" (421; Ch. 83), his still remains an exposure of the Church without parallel. That shrine of Victorian life, the family, is defiled because of the way parents become the persecutors of their own children which is the result of the excessive severity of the teaching of certain Christian groupings, the Evangelicals in particular.

The Nonconformists were in certain respects akin to the Evangelicals, but they charted an independent course for all that and largely remained outside the mainstream religious life and were somewhat distant from upper-class social life. Their primary constituencies were in the industrial North, and the story of England affected by the Industrial Revolution has as its sub-text the story of the Nonconformists or dissidents as well. Like the Evangelicals, they also set great store by reading the Scriptures and preaching among the people. But there were hardly any higher clergy in their ranks while there was no dearth of bishops among the Evangelicals. The disreputable character named Bishop who leads a rioting band of marauders in Disraeli's *Sybil* may indicate some satire at the expense of the Nonconformists. While Disraeli was a conservative, the Dissenters avowed a radical politics that was greatly feared by middle-classes and conservative politicians alike. In yet another instance of religious mockery of the pretensions of the Nonconformists, two villainous riot-leaders in Charlotte Bronte's novel *Shirley* are named Moses and Noah. While middle-class writers were generally sympathetic to the poor on the one hand and critical of various aspects of institutional Christianity on the other, they displayed a lurking fear of the mob, which was sometimes led by certain Nonconformist preachers such as the characters mentioned here.

On the whole, however, the impact of the Dissenters was positive. Their communities were dedicated and close-knit. Not being part of the establishment, they escaped the temptations of pelf and power. No wonder then that they made such deep inroads into the heart of the aggrieved, deprived populations of the industrial North, who were struggling in the nineteenth century for their rights, and for whom the divine and secular powers were hand-in-glove to throttle their aspirations. The idealised figure of Dinah Morris in George Eliot's *Adam Bede* (1859) is one of the best examples of the good that the Methodists did. Her fervent public preaching may have frightened flippant characters like Bessy: "The gentle tones, the loving persuasion, did not touch her, but when the more severe appeals came she began to be frightened" (73; Bk 1, Ch. 2). For a while Dinah also alienated the more important character called Hetty Sorrel, but unlike many other fire-and-brimstone preachers, Dinah's intention is never to scare anyone into submission. Finally, Hetty is to be transported for murdering her illegitimate newborn, and the sole saving grace is that she becomes genuinely repentant and also forgiving towards her seducer because Dinah succeeds in winning her over. Methodism is generally seen in a good light in this novel. It seems that it genuinely works on ordinary people and transforms them for the better. We are given the example of Will Maskery, a drunkard and wife-beater, who is thrifty and decent after becoming a Methodist.

The Nonconformists along with the Catholics faced restrictions and even persecution in England. However, many of the older forms of restrictions including legal disabilities and denial of admission to educational institutions started to get addressed and rectified in the reform-minded nineteenth century. The Methodists were the most visible or high profile Dissidents in this period. Writers such as Dickens and the Brontë sisters have treated them with scorn and satire, perceiving them to be too pushy and given to ranting and raving in the presence of audiences. As already indicated, they are more positively treated in *Adam Bede,* with Dinah Morris coming off as an ideal, comforting figure. On the whole, they were a powerful and substantial presence on the English landscape. John Wolffe does not exaggerate much when he says that "Dissent grew spectacularly between 1790 and 1830, thus precipitating the sense of crisis in church-state relations with which the Victorian era opened" (6).

Some people could feel threatened enough by the rise and spread of Dissent (especially because of their links to working-class agitators) to regard them as worthy of comparison to England's worst external enemies. This is indeed the viewpoint of the "kindly, peaceable" Vicar of Monkshaven in Gaskell's *Sylvia's Lovers:*

> He had two bugbears to fear – the French and the Dissenters. It was difficult to say of which he had the worst opinion and the most intense dread. Perhaps he hated the Dissenters most, because they came nearer in contact with him than the French; besides, the French had the excuse of being Papists, while the Dissenters might have belonged to the Church of England if they had not been utterly depraved". (66; Ch. 6)

Gaskell herself was a member of the unorthodox and tolerant Unitarians, and she is indulging here in a playful mockery of the divisive, non-healing role of religion. There is gentle satire at the expense of the vicar because we are told that he does not mind dining with Mr Fishburne, a friend and follower of the great Methodist leader Wesley, because the latter was a gentleman. Religion then takes a backseat to class alignments and affinities. Normally the Dissenters are associated with the poor, but Fishburne seems to be of a more genteel background and hence acceptable as a dinner-table companion.

Gaskell seems to oppose the stereotyping of all Dissenters as unruly and troublemaking by casting another Dissenter, the Quaker woman Hester, as a quiet, gentle soul. Of course, Quakers were trained to be like this, being opposed to war and slavery and following a code of equality among themselves. The quiescent Quakers or the more active Methodists alike were known for the strength of their convictions. This led them out on to the road and other public spaces, connecting with people in different ways such as leading prayer meetings and becoming missionaries. They also succeeded in making converts of people. Many lawbreakers and other outcasts of society came back to the fold heeding the appeal of Dissenting preachers and ministers. The influence of Dissent spread outside their own confines. Even liberals and unorthodox thinkers were affected by their messages.

If the Nonconformists represented a threat from below where the official Anglican Church was concerned, the leaders of the Oxford Movement could be said to be a force operating from a somewhat exclusive and privileged position, although the movement did expand and enlist a good many under its banner. As it stood against the values and principles of the Protestant Reformation, it is often called a counter-reformation. However, it was not just another episode in the battle between the High Church and Low Church factions. For the Tractarians England was becoming too worldly and turning its face away from the true, old face of religion. With typical verve (and a sense of some irony), Lytton Strachey describes the genesis of this movement: "Infidelity was stalking through the land; authority was laughed at; the hideous doctrines of Democracy was being openly preached" (12). There were also more specifically ecclesiastical, doctrinal matters that concerned people like Keble: "Worse still, if possible, the Church herself was ignorant and lukewarm; she had forgotten the mysteries of the sacraments, she had lost faith in the Apostolic Succession; she was no longer interested in the Early Fathers . . ." (12). Such issues may seem a little remote from everyday life, and it can be alleged that this movement never penetrated society the way the Evangelical crusades or the Nonconformist campaigns did. Yet in its heyday the Oxford Movement did galvanise society in its own way. To quote Strachey again, "Young men fasted and did penance, recited the hours of the Roman Breviary, and confessed their sins to

Dr. Pusey. Nor was the movement confined to Oxford; it spread in widening circles through the parishes of England: the dormant devotion of the country was suddenly aroused" (19).

The Tractarian movement left a deep imprint in Victorian culture not just because it fought for the rights of the Church assailed by secular or material forces, but also because its leading lights like Newman were splendid writers, rendering their cause memorable through letters, sermons, memoirs, and some poems and novels. Indeed, unlike the often literalistic Evangelists, the Tractarians relied on a kind of poetic style of writing to stir people's imagination. However, the movement petered out after Newman joined the Roman Catholic Church in 1845. The schism was a thing of the past; the church was in a way whole again. The affair did continue to preoccupy the minds of writers for a long time to come, though.

Newman's crossing over was in some ways a renewal of suspicions about the intentions of the Catholic Church, well-represented in England but being influenced by the Pope in distant Rome. The writings of many well-known authors in the Victorian period reflect a lingering mistrust and even hostility towards the Rome-based church. While the Catholics were a minority in England, they were only too numerous in the rest of Europe. More importantly, the Catholic faith was the official religion in France and Spain, traditional enemies of England and rivals for supremacy of various kinds in the world theatre. The historical memory of the massacres of Protestants at the hands of Catholics such as the St Bartholomew massacre (many Huguenot Protestants were killed in 1562 by Catholic assassins) may have lingered among the English Protestants, as would the memory of the terrible Thirty Years' war which ravaged large swathes of Europe in the period 1618 to 1648. Be that as it may, the case of the Catholics is an interesting one. They often brought out some of the most stinging words of condemnation from writers, sometimes in works with no overt religious thrust.

In *Shirley* the mild, lovelorn, and timorous Caroline Helstone finds space in her cogitations to spare harsh thoughts for Roman Catholicism. In the same novel there is criticism of the conduct of clergymen belonging to the Anglican and Nonconformist protestations, but in those cases it seems that the criticism is directed more against personalities rather than their ideologies. Caroline is perhaps just the mouthpiece for her creator, because in a letter written from Brussels in 1842, these are Charlotte Bronte's invectives:

> My advice to all Protestants who are tempted to do anything so besotted as turn Catholics is, to walk over the sea on to the Continent; to attend mass sedulously for a time; to note well the mummeries thereof; also the idiotic, mercenary aspect of all the priests; and then, if they are still disposed to consider Papistry in any other light than a most feeble, childish piece of humbug, let them turn Papists at once – that's all. (Qtd in Gaskell 160)

It is, however, in the final novel *Villette* that Bronte indulges in her most sustained disparagement of the Roman Catholicism, equating it with dread, supernaturalism, secretiveness and censoriousness. Charles Dickens was perhaps critical of the fanatical Lord Gordon who was responsible for the last major anti-Catholic riots in 1798, and his novel *Barnaby Rudge* (1841) is about this historical moment. In the Preface to *Barnaby Rudge* itself, he identifies himself as a man "who has no sympathy with the Romish Church." (Dickens, Preface to *Barnaby Rudge*). In *Pictures from Italy* (1846) his indictment of Catholic clergy is more explicit and devastating: "Every fourth or fifth man in the streets is a Priest or a Monk… I have no knowledge, elsewhere, of more repulsive countenances than are to be found among these gentry. If nature's handwriting, be at all legible, greater varieties of sloth, deceit, and intellectual torpor, could hardly be observed among any class of men in the world" (Dickens, "Genoa and Its Neighbourhood").

While High Church and Evangelicals could lock horns over issues such as pitched roofs in churches, and while many clergymen could caress their port, enjoy the exclusive comforts of discussing hunting and sports in the exclusive company of gentlemanly clergymen like themselves, the world with its battle-cries of reform, progress and emancipation was closing in. Reform was in the air. Of course, even before the hectic third decade of the century, the serenity of the clerical establishment was ruffled by the cannonades of the French Revolution. Towards the middle of the century reform acquired a dynamism and an urgency that was irresistible. Of course, it would be a while before the Church would truly be congenial towards agnostics or non-believers. Religious tests for admission to the great universities of Cambridge and Oxford would also be abolished only in 1871. As the late century novels of Thomas Hardy testify, the clerical establishment never yielded its rights and privileges completely or willingly.

Religious trends which were in a state of flux in the Victorian period drew out a whole range of literary responses from writers. Many of these writers found themselves responding to religious issues even though their main concerns may not have had anything to do with church affairs or the ways of God. The sprawling form of the novel demanded an engagement with the different rhythms of existence in a rapidly secularising world, and religion could rarely be focused upon to the exclusion of other things. Many of the Victorian poets, however, often chose overtly religious subjects. They frequently drew inspiration from the popularity of the hymns and prayers which reached broad sections of society. There were poets like Christina Rossetti and Tennyson who occasionally lapsed into a prayer mode themselves in many of their poems.

However, even among poets (including the two mentioned above) there was variety. There were shades of nuanced responses that fell between sceptical rejections or anguished loss of faith on the one hand, and on the other, uncritical embracement of the positions of official Christianity. Religion was a subject of literary *explorations*, and the various subjects stimulated them to write differently and innovatively. Gerard Manley Hopkins's technical ingenuity is as remarkable as the depth of his religious intensity, so much so, that he is often read as a modern rather than a Victorian poet. Even Robert Browning is exemplary in this regard for his wide-ranging and eclectic confrontation with matters which were religious, but which had worldly implications as well. His composite vision entailed mixing up profound Christian tenets with his secular preoccupations with love (or man–woman relations in general) and art.

Essentially a believer in God's goodness and rightness, Browning's famous optimism was reassuringly congruent with prevailing orthodox beliefs. A poem such as "Rabbi Ben Ezra" exemplifies the robust, positive aspect of Christian conviction. To evoke God's creativity and caring nature, Browning repeatedly uses the model and metaphor of the potter and the potter's wheel in this poem. This more organic response reminds us of the image of God as a clockmaker which was prevalent in the mechanical, Deistic universe of eighteenth-century philosophical thought: "Earth changes, but thy soul and God stand sure:/What entered into thee, /That was, is, and shall be: Time's wheel runs back or stops: Potter and clay endure" (ll. 159–62).

Relating the potter's wheel to the wheel of life itself, Browning finds himself reaching an end that is a satisfactory culmination in a both artistic and religious sense: "My times be in Thy hand! Perfect the cup as planned! /Let age approve of youth, and death complete the same!" (ll.190–92) Life on this earth not perfect, and men's time is not only finite, but also marked by the frailties of flesh (an issue Browning investigates in the well-known "religious" poem "Fra Lippo Lippi").

The belief in the certainty of God's concern and creativity is also in the poem "A Death in the Desert", a poem about the apostle John. As F. B. Pinion points out in his annotative commentary, "It contains one of the most central tenets of Browning's faith: God is love, and his love was revealed to men through Christ" (Robert Browning 191).

Neither this particular poem nor Browning's religious poetic oeuvre can be reduced to a reading about loving kindness, however. In his poems that deal partly or wholly with religious issues, Browning seems as much concerned with the varied nature of human experiences as about the certainty and absoluteness of divine benevolence. As poems such as "Fra Lippo Lippi" testify, Browning seemed to take creative delight in human frailties as well as in human imperfection. He also admits doubts and uncertainties, making reference to the contemporary debate about the literal truth of the Scriptures and to Broad Church–High Church clashes on doctrinal matters. One remembers in this regard that Browning was under the influence of the atheistic Shelley. While his may not be the last word, the doubting unorthodox Christian Cerinthus is given an important role in the poem "A Death in the Desert." The always-dramatic Browning indulges in an interplay of conflicting religious opinions through the creation of such characters.

Like the novelists, poets of the period often thematised the contemporary crisis of faith and the necessity of granting a hearing to the voices of doubt. Apart from Cerinthus there is the speaker of the revealingly titled poem "Unfaith and Faith" who seems to voice precisely this quality which has crept into the religious discourse of the time:

> Why first, you don't believe, you don't and can't
> (Not statedly, that is, and fixedly
> And Absolutely and exclusively)
> In any revelation called divine.

...
All we've gained is, that belief,
As unbelief before, shakes us by fits,
Confounds us like its predecessors. (ll. 1–30)

Arthur H. Clough is another poet who introduces a note of satire and scepticism into the territory of faith and belief. This is how his well-known poem "The Latest Decalogue" goes: "Thou shall have one God only: who would be at the expense of two? ... No graven images may be Worshipped, except the currency: ... Do not adultery commit; Advantage rarely comes of it. Thou shall not steal; an empty feat, When it's so lucrative to cheat; (ll. 1–16)

But like Browning Clough was also a believer. He may be poking fun here at the people with their unholy, material attitude, an attitude which was partly responsible for religion itself getting tarnished in the Victorian period, thereby distorting the message of Christianity.

More heartfelt and devout are the religious poems of Christina Rossetti. She can be held up as a model of conventional faith, always singing the Lord's praise with an ardent heart. However, in her case too one will find issues that go beyond simple affirmation marked by some pain and anguish.

As we have seen, Christianity was no monolith, and it is interesting to see shades of conflict or opposition between different schools of belief. Religion also lent its tropes, images, and vocabulary to writers who might be dealing with non-religious or secular subjects. In the words of John Wolffe, "Religious ideologues could cloak secular objectives, just as secular ideologies could be pursued with quasi-religious intensity" (9). Religious meaning could thus be extended, and religion could ensure its own survival by becoming available for secular "uses."

The Brontës, both in their poetry (one is thinking particularly of Emily here) and in their fiction, exemplify this "use" of religion in this particular sense. As in her fiction, critics discern an alternative religious world in Emily's poetry also. There seems to be religious fervour and intensity, but not the forms of official Christianity. Also, the heart's yearnings are as much, if not more evident, than prayerful supplication to God in poems such as "No Coward Soul is Mine."

It is Charlotte's *Villette* (1853), the writer's last novel, that best exemplifies how one best addresses the emerging issues of women's psychological/inner struggles and vocational/identitarian achievements in the existing language of Christianity. Giving examples of the choice of biblical phrases as well as of Christian motifs and myths (such as that of the martyr) from the novel, John Maynard says: "*Villette* continues to work within the language and culture of Christianity, even as it focuses more constantly on the secular destiny of one woman" (209). A little later he says: "Indeed in *Villette* the work is most often the work of recycling traditional religious mythic language into a language to describe not existence and metaphysics, the outside world, but psychology, the inside world" (210).

The Brontës have been regarded as eccentric, rebellious, outcast figures, and their critiques, subversions, and reinterpretations of religious notions and templates are actually in keeping with their characters, notwithstanding the fact that they were daughters of a clergyman. However, in the more straightforwardly pious Christina Rossetti one can see camouflaged religion serving secular concerns. Her notable work, *Goblin Market,* tempts one to come up with religious interpretations regarding the forbidden fruit or the body of Christ. However, there is nothing direct or overt. The veiled nature of religious ideas is in keeping with the psychological, suggestive character of the poem. It is a poem written by an earnestly religious writer who explores complex issues of women's bonding and even sexual relations between women. The secular and the religious are mixed up here, which may be regarded as a trend for the future.

Before closing the subject, another aspect of Victorian religion will be very briefly touched upon here, meaning the activities of the missionaries. Britain sent out missionaries belonging to different denominations – Catholic and Protestant, Jesuit and Baptist, Nonconformist and Anglican Church of England. Many of them were from Ireland, Wales and Scotland. Quite a few of them were also from the working-classes, providing an indication of how religion was both vocation and career in nineteenth-century England. This was the period when the maximum expansion of Christianity took place on the global map through the outward forays of missionaries from the West. According to T. Thomas,

> The number of foreign missionaries from Britain and Ireland equalled the number of accountants and architects in employment in these countries. There were half as many missionaries as there were Anglican priests and three times as many missionaries as Roman Catholic clergy in Britain and Ireland. The British missionary societies and agencies spent annually £2.000, 000, equivalent to 2 per cent of government expenditure, and as much as the total salaries of the entire civil service. (Wolffe 103–04)

A lot has been written about the missionaries and their activities and achievements. The missionaries themselves (and sometimes their wives) have also left behind voluminous writings about their sojourns in different lands. In Victorian literature the most famous missionary is perhaps St John Rivers in *Jane Eyre* (1847). Rivers and Rochester are the two men in Jane's life, and it seems that Brontë projects them as two alternatives for the heroine. He is part of that great missionary boom which animated the mid-Victorian religious and political landscape. One says political because the missionaries were an important cog in the imperial machinery which sought to downgrade the cultural and religious practices of the colonised and impose its own instead. Indeed, John Maynard calls him "this 'pioneer' missionary imperialist" (204). However, what is important in the context of this chapter is whether Rivers, and through him, Christianity itself, is under some scrutiny or not. Conventionally the missionaries were noble and self-sacrificing as well as altruistic. But does pride and egoism spur them on? Maynard hints at the possibility of a critical reading of the role of the missionary as a patriarchal figure (Christianity certainly is a very patriarchal religion):

> The novel inscribes . . . ambivalence about Christianity and religious *men* [emphasis Maynard's] on its final page, as Jane tells us, in language that may be, or may not be taken as ironic (irony being a trope in the eyes of the beholder), of the celibate missionary's assurance of 'his sure reward, his incorruptible crown' [these are words from the text of *Jane Eyre*]. (204)

Thus, as an appraisal of the social and cultural history of Victorian England as well as an engagement with the actual works of literary artists reveal, Christianity had a rocky journey, battling external foes and having to come to terms with diverse and dissenting perspectives and standpoints within its own fold. The popularity of Christianity as an entire mode of being, a master narrative that moulds or recasts behavioural patterns and impacts desires and aspirations, also recedes somewhat in the face of competition from other lifestyle modes. Many thinkers and creative writers of the period felt impelled to tread the path of open-minded enquiry in the atmosphere of reform and scientific discovery. Of course, such progressive attitudes were not acceptable to the resistant forces clinging to the past, but there was no stopping progress.

Religion was a solemn subject, literally a matter of life and death for many people. To think of religion was to think of human mortality. However, unlike scientists for whom death was mainly extinction, religion reached out to or worried about life beyond death. Many sought comfort in the thought of a benign deity under whose wings a happy time of eternity could be spent. The overall preoccupation with religion resulted in Victorian culture acquiring an overtly moral varnish and veneer. The unswerving fixation on this or that aspect of Christian dogma and doctrine leads to a sectarian narrowness and a moral, judgemental severity that writers as diverse as Dickens, Trollope, Eliot, Lewis Carroll and Hardy undermine. The "pluralist" Reverend Irwin could be speaking for many of them when he tells Adam Bede in Eliot's novel of that name: "It is not for us men to apportion the shares of moral guilt and retribution. We find it impossible to avoid mistakes even in determining who has committed a single criminal act, and the problem how far a man is to be held responsible for the unforeseen consequences of his own deed, is one that might well make us tremble to look into it" (468; Bk 5, Ch. 41). As quotations such as these indicate, in their subtlety and perceptiveness the best of the Victorians from Browning to Eliot and Hardy realised that unlike what religious orthodoxy would have people believe, morality was a complex affair, and good and evil were not clearly separable: in fact, they were sometimes embedded in the same individual.

The fact was that Victorian morality nurtured by the more intolerant religious formations such as the Evangelists was at the same time a matter of public discourse and rhetoric. The moralists harangued and hectored the populace to tread the path of virtue. Considering that there was so much of a moral intervention from the public sphere, the dangers of succumbing to various temptations in private while going along with the official slogans of morality was very much a possibility. Dickens's wonderful gallery of moral hypocrites from Pecksniff to Casby is a reflection of this reality. The pressure to be pure and moral also meant that the Victorians could not be as explicit or graphic about many sordid or unsavoury aspects of existence such as the problems of prostitutes and the threat of venereal disease.

As already stated, the increasingly liberal tendencies of the age ensured that the Calvinistic or Evangelical emphasis on sin and retribution gradually decreased. For some a new dispensation of hope seemed to be a possibility. In the somewhat colourful language of Boyd Hilton, "in the Church of England, that is in comfortable upper and middle-class circles, the image of God was changing – from that of a fierce headmaster proclaiming that vengeance was his – to that of a sort of Santa Claus" (237). However, with the shadows of modern existence lengthening, it would be perhaps increasingly less a case of a kind God replacing a hard God than God disappearing altogether. Thoughts of either eternal damnation or eternal salvation would not be easily sustainable in a post-Darwinian world. The various corollaries of the evolutionary paradigm were making nonsense of the providential interpretation of life on earth. Actually what happened to Christianity cannot be understood without a due consideration of the triumphant march of science, and it is to this that we turn in the next chapter.

Works Cited

Bentley, Phyllis. *The Brontës.* London: Thames and Hudson, 1997. Print.

Biagini, E. F. "Radicalism and Liberty." *Liberty and Authority in Victorian Britain.* Ed. Peter Mandler. Oxford: Oxford UP, 2006. 101–24. Print.

Boyd, Hilton, "Religion, Doctrine and Public Policy." *The Victorian Studies Reader.* Eds. Kelly Boyd and Rohan McWilliam. London and New York: Routledge, 2007. 235–43. Print.

Brontë, Charlotte. *Shirley.* London: Penguin Books, 2012. Print. The Penguin English Library.

Brontë, Emily. *Wuthering Heights.* Ware, Herfordshire: Wordsworth Editions Limited, 1992. Print. Wordsworth Classics.

Browning, Robert. "Rabbi Ben Ezra." *Robert Browning: Dramatis Personae.* Ed. F. B. Pinion. Glasgow and London: Collins Publishers, 1969. 63–70. Print.

Butler, Samuel. *The Way of All Flesh.* London: Jonathan Cape, 1948. Print.

Clough, Arthur Hugh. "The Latest Decalogue." *The Faber Book of Religious Verse.* Ed. Helen Gardner. London: Faber and Faber, 1972. 267. Print.

Davis, Philip. *The Victorians. The Oxford English Literary History: Volume 8: 1830–1880.* Oxford: Oxford UP, 2002. Print.

Dickens, Charles. *Pictures from Italy.* Project Gutenberg e-book. 23 March 2015. <http://www.gutenberg.org/ebooks>.

———. *Barnaby Rudge.* Project Gutenberg e-book. 18 April 2015. <http://www.gutenberg.org/ebooks>

———. *The Old Curiosity Shop.* Oxford: Oxford UP, 1998. Print. Oxford World's Classics.

———. *Hard Times.* Oxford: Oxford UP, 1989. Print. Oxford World's Classics.

———. *Great Expectations.* London and Glasgow: Collins, 1953. Print.

———. *Little Dorrit.* Oxford: Oxford UP, 1991. Print. Oxford World's Classics.

Eliot, George. *Adam Bede.* Harmondsworth, Middlesex, England: Penguin Books, 1987. Print. Penguin Classics.

Gaskell, Elizabeth. *Sylvia's Lovers.* Oxford: Oxford UP, 2008. Print. World's Classics.

———. The *Life of Charlotte Bronte.* London and Melbourne: J. M. Dent, 1984. Print. Everyman's Library.

Herbert, Christopher. *Trollope and Comic Pleasure.* Chicago: Chicago UP, 1987. Print.

Maynard, John. "The Brontës and Religion." *The Cambridge Companion to the Brontës.* Ed. Heather Glen. Cambridge: Cambridge UP, 2002. 192–213. Print.

Strachey, Lytton. "Cardinal Manning." *Eminent Victorians.* Radford VA: Wilder Publications, 2008. 7–83. Print.

Thomas, T. "Foreign Missions and Missionaries in Victorian Britain." *Religion in Victorian Britain: Volume V Culture and Empire.* Ed. John Wolffe. Manchester: Manchester UP, 1997. 101–34. Print.

Trollope, Anthony. *Barchester Towers.* Harmondsworth, Middlesex, England: Penguin Books, 1984. Print. The Penguin English Library.

Wheeler, Michael. *Heaven, Hell and the Victorians.* Cambridge: Cambridge UP, 1990. Print.

Wolffe, John. "Introduction: Victorian Religion in Context." *Religion in Victorian Britain: Volume V Culture and Empire.* Ed. John Wolffe. Manchester: Manchester UP, 1997. 1–20. Print.

TWO

Darwin and Others

The Triumphant March of Science

While science probably caused a great deal of harm to the cause of religion and eroded its sovereignty, there were attempts to find common ground in times prior to the Victorian era and also during it. Interestingly enough, many theologians also dabbled in science. One well-known pre-Victorian example is William Paley, an optimistic eighteenth-century philosopher and theologian who, apart from defending Christianity, thought and wrote about evolution – the science that would change the world more irrevocably for religious people than any other discipline. As Philip Davis points out,

> Cooperation between science and religion had reached its peak in the 1830s with the publication of the Bridgewater treatises, when the eighth Earl of Bridgewater had commissioned separate treatises on astronomy, physics, geology, and on animal, vegetable, and human physiology – all in relation to the goodness of God as their connecting origin. (57)

What many such people wished to highlight was the wondrousness, beauty, symmetry and intricacy that one found in nature. The flowers and trees, valleys and dales, rivers and waterfalls – all bore the impress of a master craftsman at work. This was the core of the Deistic philosophy of the eighteenth century, but in the more insecure and anxious nineteenth century also such an argument found all-too ready hearers. An acute need was felt to posit a sense of purpose and design behind all natural phenomena, and identify an author who breathed down benignly on the world.

However, the telos sought by divines and religiously inclined artists were under serious threat in the evolutionary nineteenth century. While science was an "industry" that buzzed and hummed in radical classrooms, laboratories and factories, the insights gained from scientific voyages and expeditions were instrumental in dislodging humans (and God) from the centre of the scheme of things. Such a voyage was the one made by Charles Darwin in the ship called *Beagle*. The voyage on the *Beagle* lasted for five years and it took Charles Darwin to the ends of the earth, climaxing in remote Galagapos Archipelago off the coast of Ecuador. This region was a wonderful living laboratory of organisms, the study of which proved to be extremely fruitful in the shaping of evolutionary theories. Before reaching this place, Darwin saw different races by observing whom he started giving mental shape to his crucial notions of variability and survival. Darwin studied different kinds of books, including works by Milton. He kept notes as the voyage progressed, seeing many new plant and animal species, and produced more notes after returning home based on some of which he wrote the work called *The Journal of Research* the first version of which appeared in 1839. He continued to develop the theory of the evolution of the species, taking his time until the knowledge of similar work being done by Alfred Russell Wallace drove him into a hurried completion of the epoch-making *The Origin of Species* (1859). After the publication of this work, all the old remaining certainties were gone. Suddenly men were no longer confident that they were guided to a celestial destination, "that far-off divine event to whole creation moves," (a phrase from "In Memoriam" by Tennyson) by an unseen but caring hand.

Even for a person far removed from the English scientific scene, "Darwin" rings a bell. 'Darwinian' is an adjective that encompasses a whole world and expresses a worldview that brings in a sense of the radical irreversibility of knowledge. That is to say, the world may actually be divided into pre-Darwin and post-Darwin when we consider the origin of life and the human's place in nature. But Darwin did not work in isolation and his work did not emerge from just anywhere. He benefited from work done in his field by many others, some of whom belonged to the previous era. In fact, as Gillian Beer points out in her introduction to an edition of *The Origin of Species,* "these diverse elements, fruitful for evolutionary thinking, were already available and under discussion in intellectual and activist circles, some from long before Darwin was born and all before he was a grown man" ("Introduction" xi).

Many writers who can loosely be identified as evolutionary thinkers were on the scene before Darwin. Some of them had started thinking about evolution as early as the fifth century B.C., according to John Gribbin and Michael White (27). There would be many others after those pioneers who would ponder on various evolving or mutating life forms, from an antique age. Darwin's debt to them would vary according to where their areas of emphases lay as well as the viability of their theses and the depth of their scholarship. However, these writers (some of them writing just a little before the Victorian era began) were instrumental in bringing evolutionary thinking to the mental radar of the Victorians as their works were often re-published. In turn they provoked or inspired creative writers to come up with works inflected with ideas pertaining to the origin of species, their propagation, and their extinction. Charles Lyell is one of those pioneering writers. Tennyson, among others, read his work closely and incorporated some of his ideas in "In Memoriam", a poem whose initial sections are saturated with geological images and evolutionary thoughts. Lyell was preceded by writers such as Jean Lamarck and Robert Chambers.

Among these pre-Darwinian works chronologically only Chambers' *Vestiges of Creation* (1844) falls within the Victorian period. However, the works of the other two writers also shaped Victorian thinking in this regard. Chambers was an amateur, one of those who contributed to and perhaps also benefited from the popularity of science in the period. The French writer Lamarck was a more learned figure. Today he is remembered chiefly in relation to Darwin. Lamarck made an important point about the impact of the environment on living bodies or organisms. He also pointed out that while there was a chain of being, starting at a lower point and then going on to a higher, more perfect form, this progression was not necessarily very smooth or regular. This was already a cautious anticipation of future theories which would postulate that while evolution was a "progressive" and linear affair and seemed to follow certain laws, there might be an element of unpredictability about it. There were other Lamarckian insights regarding inheritance and transformation which would be taken up by later scientists such as Darwin and which would have a bearing on the development of evolutionary science. Darwin followed up with acuter, more refined, and often less comforting insights.

Lyell wrote his influential and controversial *Principles of Geology* in 1830. His was one of the first refutations of what is called the Mosaic (deriving from Moses the prophet whose story appears in the *Old Testament*) or Creationist view of the coming into being of this earth and its inhabitants. By no means an irreligious man, Lyell however argued that the world came about not through the swift or "catastrophic" intervention of God, but through the operation of slow and regular causes which were visible or prevalent even in the present. Like Lamarck, Lyell also seems concerned with the relationship between the creature and its environment. However, he downplays the role of humans who, he believed, had no greater impact on the environment than did other animals. Important as Lyell's insights were for evolutionary science right from the beginning, he did not consider himself to be an evolutionist for a long time. In the words of Jonathan Howard, "the greatest evolutionary geologist of the age dismissed all evolutionary biology until he was finally convinced that Darwin had indeed found a valid mechanism for the evolutionary process" (23). This quotation underscores the importance of Darwin in consolidating the speculations of earlier thinkers and giving those speculations and hypotheses a finishing touch that would change the whole business of science as people understood it. In the words of Gribbin and White, Darwin "was not the first person to think about evolution. He was not even the first member of his own family to think about evolution. But he was the first person to come up with a theory of evolution that proved able to withstand rigorous scientific testing" (27).

The thought of people such as Lyell and Darwin decentred humans from the scheme of things. They were believers rather than agnostics and atheists. Yet, the divine being understood primarily in relation to its effect on man, the diminishment of human beings resulting from their explorations also resulted in a certain marginalisation of the divine. Many of the non-human insights dealing primarily with the birds, animals and insects seemed to be analogically transferable to the human condition. It is not as if the human race suddenly ceased to be of significance. It is just that human motive, behaviour and history were now readable from new perspectives. Human beings were now compelled to reconsider their place in the scheme of things and newer facets of human identity would emerge as a result. The fact was that the human was also an *animal,* and would share the fates and experiences of other animals.

Like other evolutionary thinkers, Lyell also trained his guns on the reassuring contemporary interpretations on survival and extinction. Extinction was as much a part of life as productivity or proliferation. Such extinction was attributable partly to what would become famous in Darwin's hands as the struggle for existence. Lyell believed that species in a country were at war with each other and this led to extinction on a large scale.

When one talks about extinction especially in relation to the struggle for survival, a non-evolutionary, pre-Victorian thinker such as Thomas Malthus must also be considered, particularly because of his influence on Darwin. Malthus's legacy was rather bleak and the echoes of his thought can also be heard in literary works which steadfastly look at the harsher aspects of life. Thomas Malthus was indeed an extraordinary influence on Darwin as well as on many creative writers of subsequent generations. To put it somewhat dramatically, the shadow of this man of religion who could hold out very few hopes to humankind hovered over the nineteenth century, and extended into the twentieth century and beyond. After all, no age can be free of the anxiety and urgency of the capacity for survival in the face of limited resources and burgeoning populations. In the Victorian period itself, one of the fears about the poor – that they were sexually unrestrained and bred prolifically in their hovels and shanties – seems a rather Malthusian fear. In Hardy's late Victorian novel, *Jude the Obscure* (1896), the child-character named Father Time, after expressing dismay at an impending birth in the family and then killing his step-siblings due to the parents' poverty-related struggles, makes the poignant but horrifying Malthusian statement: "Done because we are too menny" (410; Pt. 6, Bk 2).

For this was what Malthus's core finding amounted to: a population that increased or multiplied geometrically (two becomes four, four becomes sixteen, and so on) while the earth's resources could not keep pace with such accelerating numbers. The Biblical injunction to be fruitful and multiply received a somewhat negative interpretation at Malthus's hands. Malthus forced many to consider that the celebratory and creative phenomenon called the propagation of species could carry in it the seeds of misery and tragedy. The ramifications of his vision reached late into the nineteenth century and beyond, finding echoes in works such as *Jude the Obscure* and the works of George Gissing where the individual travail reflects a larger reality.

This is the right time to summarise Darwin's own thoughts and contributions, as his ideas became powerful tropes for Victorian writers with a gamut of diverse dispositions and writing ambitions and agendas. One of his more seminal concepts is the struggle for survival. Many of the other ideas such as variability, reproduction, the birth of new species and extinction of parent species may be seen to cluster around this key concept which had a powerful appeal to writers working in an age of intense conflict and competition. While formulating this notion, Darwin acknowledges his debt to Thomas Malthus.

In the chapter on struggle, Darwin begins by talking about things like adaptation and survival and also of variation that can aid in survival. Then he invokes Malthus to lay out the full implications of the struggle for survival:

> Every being, which during its natural lifetime produces several eggs or seeds, must suffer destruction during some period of its life, and during some season or occasional year, otherwise, on the principle of geometrical increase, its numbers would quickly become so inordinately great that no country could support the product. Hence, as more individuals are produced than can possibly survive, there must in every case be a struggle for existence, either one individual with another of the same species, or with the individuals of distinct species, or with the physical conditions of life. It is the doctrine of Malthus applied with manifold force to the whole animal and vegetable kingdom; for in this case there can be no artificial increase of food, and no prudential restraint from marriage. (53–54)

While this may be specifically with reference to the non-human world, the human is not too far away because Darwin goes on to add:

> There is no exception to the rule that every organic being naturally increases at so high rate, that if not destroyed, the earth would soon be covered by the progeny of a single pair. Even slow-breeding man has doubled in twenty-five years, and at this rate, in a few thousand years, there would literally not be standing room for his progeny. (54)

Darwin's was actually a balanced estimate of how things stood regarding creation and destruction/extinction. The struggle that he talks about while invoking Malthus (and that seemed to have exerted such fascination not just on the Victorian mind but also on later generations), is duly inclusive of the destruction that is rife in this world. At one point Darwin actually seems to warn one against an optimistic or sentimental reading of nature:

> We behold the face of nature bright with gladness, we often see superabundance of food; we do not see, or we forget that the birds which are idly singing round us mostly live on insects or seeds, and are thus constantly destroying life; or we forget how largely these songsters, or their eggs, or their nestlings, are destroyed by birds and beasts of prey; we do not always bear in mind, that though food may be now superabundant, it is not so at all seasons of each recurring year. (53)

If these are the most striking lines about extinction in all of Darwin, there are other places too where he mentions it.

It is possible then to talk about the positive and the negative in Darwin, to moments of celebration as well as of lamentation. However, he sees proliferation/production and extinction/destruction as inseparable and almost complementary ideas. The simple fact is that not everyone or everything can survive. At the same time, species *will* want to increase their numbers at any cost. This very attempt to increase numbers, however, may bring in extinction. The universal principle of productivity/proliferation will bring in its wake extinction or extermination on a large scale.

Darwin introduced a note of great impersonality into the proceedings (an attitude that today we would call "scientific" or objective). The contemplation of the ongoing drama of life brings home the lesson that neither the divine nor its surrogate the human is at work and superintending affairs. For the nineteenth century, attributing concern for the human race or for all creatures to God was comforting. We remember Tennyson's fond hope in this context: "That not a worm is cloven in vain; /That not a moth with vain desire/ Is shrivel'd in a fruitless fire" (Canto LIII, ll. 9–12). If the direct hand of God was not always visible at least a persuasion that human agency was meaningful could be reassuring. Lamarck's example of the giraffe stretching its neck to elongate it was popular – such ideas were always transferable and went along with the belief in individual effort that was so characteristic of Victorian thought.

But Darwin would have none of that. He formulated his most potent concept, Natural Selection, that rejects both benevolent intervention by the Creator (God) and simple volition on the part of the Creature, either human or non-human. Natural Selection was a kind of neutral force within nature. A description such as the following would be disturbing to the Victorian mind which greatly valorised the ideal of motherhood: "maternal love or maternal hatred, though the latter fortunately is most rare, is all the same to the inexorable principle of natural selection"(Darwin 165). He is actually talking about a practice that is for the welfare of the community, in this case the practice of the queen bees, to destroy her daughters or herself perish in the attempt. It may be mentioned here that Darwin rather interestingly characterises Nature as feminine.

Natural Selection is a force that preserves those traits or features that is of help to the organism in its drive for survival. It is something that tends towards perfection although there is at times an acknowledgement on Darwin's part that absolute perfection is rare in nature. Darwin also sees different variations in a species at different stages and Natural Selection *accumulates* (this is a key word because nothing is miraculous or instantaneous) the variations that are of use. Natural Selection may also check tendencies towards further variations if they are not of any use.

At times Darwin stresses the benign aspect of Natural Selection. Compared to Artificial Selection (undertaken by the human being who wants to improve plants or domestic animals under his care), Natural Selection is more generous. Man only regards his own personal benefit or welfare when he is engaged in artificial selection. However, Natural Selection is concerned for the entire species. Yet there is justification in seeing it as a not very comforting concept as Tennyson indeed did in his more pessimistic and honest moments: "So careful of the type she seems,/So careless of the single life; . . . . And finding that of fifty seeds/She often brings but one to bear" (Tennyson LIV, ll. 7–12). While every species is helped in the preservation of useful traits by Natural Selection, the fact remains that these species engage in the struggle for life in an arena which is not theirs alone but is inhabited by competing species.

Darwin's work, involving minute observations of plant and animal kingdoms, did stress plenitude and proliferation. Life forms grew and evolved – obviously in the direction of some kind of perfection. As he worried over the distinction between species and variety, diversity of life was highlighted. However, he also drew attention to mutation, extinction, and even a certain randomness. Nature, which in an earlier habit of thinking, seemed to carry the impress of God's artistry and concern, now became cruel in its indifference. Indifferent, and yet arbitrary rather than fixed and reassuring as the following lines from *The Mayor of Casterbridge* attests: "The difference between the peacefulness of inferior nature and the wilful hostilities of mankind was very apparent at this place . . . there was a natural instinct to abjure man as the blot on an otherwise kindly universe; till it was remembered that all terrestrial conditions were intermittent, and that mankind might some night be innocently sleeping when these quiet objects were raging loud" (14; Vol. 1, Ch. 1). While it is Hardy who among Victorian authors seems most preoccupied with a somewhat whimsical or malign indifference of "mother" nature, it is again Tennyson whose words are most quoted in this regard: "Tho' Nature, red in tooth and claw/ With ravine, shriek'd against his creed" (LV, ll. 15–16).

Darwin posits the notion of the web: every creature or every species lives in relation to every other species. He talks about the "condition of life" (what today we may loosely call the environment) and also concedes that it may have an impact. Organisms may need to adapt to their environments. However, it is clear to the scientist that more than the condition of life (climate, geography etc.) it is the existence and action of other species that is of greater consequence, apart from various invisible laws at work. We can see how such a notion – of leading intricately connected lives, sometimes marked by conflicts of interest – would gain a grip on Victorian writers from Dickens to Hardy. In George Eliot there is an implicit warning to be careful in what one does, because our actions could affect people in ways that we cannot conceive or imagine. Of course, every creature has a Darwinian instinct for self-preservation, the kind that finds memorable expression in Hardy's *Tess of the D'Urbervilles:* "some spirit within her rose automatically as the sap in the twigs. It was unexpended youth, surging up anew after its temporary check, and bringing with it hope, and the invincible instinct towards self-delight" (104; Ph. 2, Ch. XV). However, unlike Tess herself, the instinct of many other characters is to take an advantage over others. No wonder then that Tess fails in the race of life, exploited by others, and falls by the wayside.

This last is a Malthusian observation, and in this essay I have already shown Darwin's debt to the earlier thinker. However, Darwin went beyond Malthus, and it can be argued that he erected a more optimistic structure of thought on the earlier writer's pessimistic thesis. Darwin was fascinated by reproduction and productivity, plenitude, proliferation and progression. As Gillian Beer points out in her seminal work, *Darwin's Plots,* "To Malthus fecundity was a danger to be suppressed [Malthus begins his work with a vision of fecundity or fertility, as Beer points out] – particularly by draconian measures among the poor. To Darwin fecundity was a liberating and creative principle, leading to increased variability, increased potential for change and development" (29). While such a comparison is fair and accurate enough, Darwin as much as Malthus shows, through his researches, the world as a contested arena, hosting a struggle for existence. Also, in his application of the same theories and principles regarding fertility or survival that one would use for the study of plants and animals to the case of human beings, Malthus was a pioneer figure. For Malthus as for scientists like Lyell and Darwin, man's life seemed encompassed by animal categories of breeding, food-seeking and perishing. One can find examples for this animal fate of human beings in the canonical literature of the Victorian period. The many parallels shown between Hardy's protagonists and various birds or animals attest to the presence of stark scientific attitudes behind the portrayal of emotional scenes. The dying birds that Tess takes pity on in the novel named after her have failed in the race of life. Also, their fate looks forward to Tess's own destiny. In *Jude the Obscure* the eponymous hero looks at certain birds in the field and feels that like him they seemed to be living in a world that did not want them.

Darwin lays great emphasis on descent and inheritance. The trait or variation that is not passed on or not inherited is of no value. Darwin's ideas also resonated in the Victorian context because Victorian narratives were family-centred, and were preoccupied with issues of family likeness, resemblance, difference, and generally, with the bloodline or the family line. Works as diverse as *Wuthering Heights, Vanity Fair* and *The Mill on the Floss* are stories of generations where the reader finds herself paying close attention to the traits and characteristics that may be inherited from an ancestor and that may have a decisive bearing on the course of the narrative. In a novel such as *Wuthering Heights* (1847) there is also a familiar struggle for existence. However, it is within families; this reminds us of Darwin's observations about how the main struggle is within a species rather than between different species. Darwin, along with other evolutionists, may have decentred the human, but the human makes a return through the dynamics of Darwinian narratives such as *Wuthering Heights* and *Vanity Fair* (with its marine cannibal image applied to a character such as Becky Sharp) which show how precarious so-called civilisation is, how red nature still "survives" in humans.

Another very interesting interpretation of Darwin's struggle as applied through family motifs and familial modes of behaviour can be seen in Charles Kingsley's *The Water Babies* (1862). Kingsley was one of those men of religion who were fascinated by the wonders of science. This work is classic Victorian family reading, meant for children. It does not depict the usual domesticity, but the presence of people like Mrs Bedonebyasyoudid, Mrs Doasyouwouldbedoneby and Mother Carey do strike a family note, apart from the hint of romance between Tom and Ellie, and the very idea of babies, of whatever form. The work is amplified through references to the work of scientists and the evolutionary notion of extinction.

Yet another extension of Darwinian notions of extinction and survival can be seen in the privileged role attributed to the demise and persistence of the past in writers such as Hardy. The past had vanished, and while geological records of the past such as fossils were not always easy to read or retrieve, it was realised that they were scattered throughout present-day civilisation. Thomas Hardy seemed particularly fascinated by the role that the past played – it cropped up in the lives of people, lingered, haunted the characters. Often, long buried and hidden objects symbolise the past as something lying dormant, sedimented over, waiting discovery. Such an object is the Roman soldier who is unearthed in *The Mayor of Casterbridge*. This is a novel where the past has particular potency. It lays waste the lives of those like Michael Henchard and Lucetta who would ignore or suppress the past.

For writers such as Hardy, antiquarian interests combine with scientific curiosity and knowledge to create dramatic effects. Unlike in the picaresque fiction of the previous era – whereby things, places, and characters are left quite permanently behind in the linear progress of the narrative, Victorian literature displays an acute interest in the continuity and persistency of things, something perhaps born of scientific awareness regarding how past knowledge is necessary to make sense of the present and prepare for the future.

A dominant form in the Victorian period was the bildungsroman. The cornerstone of the bildungsroman (some well-known examples being *David Copperfield, Great Expectations, Vanity fair, Jane Eyre, Villette,* and the more ironically treated *Adventures of Harry Richmond and The Ordeal of Richard Feverel* by George Meredith and *The Way of All Flesh* by Samuel Butler) is change. Change was of course at the heart of the Darwinian project, in the form of variability and mutability, as well as in Lyell's thesis about the evolution of the earth. However, these writers pointed to slow change as against the catastrophist nature of the Creationist view. The pace of the bildungsroman tallied with the vision of the evolutionists. In the examples mentioned above, characters *evolve,* – over fairly long periods of time. We see them from birth or childhood to adulthood and maturity, and whatever changes they undergo come about through numerous encounters and contacts with people and events. The narratives of the lives of these people is like the narrative of the planet itself. The keyword is cumulative.

Whether it is the scientific idea that is uppermost in the writer's mind, or whether s/he is simply concerned to wring out emotional mileage from such moments, it is undeniable that there was a growing recognition that it was a remorseless world of struggle and defeat for numerous species and individuals. The trappings or outer glosses of civilisation or culture, such as clothes, fine manners and language, music, and good-looking homes only hid or postponed the reality. The reality was that humans were born like animals, and often met the fate of animals – for all their vaunted superiority over the beasts of the field and the birds of the heavens.

As Laura Otis points out, the word "science" used in the modern sense came into existence only in the 1830s (xvii), and it is there that we have to put down a marker when assessing Darwin's inheritance. In the year 1831, the British Association for the Advancement of Science was formed. Even Darwin's path-breaking voyage in the *Beagle* was not one of a kind. As William Irvine points out, the nineteenth century was the heroic age for scientific voyages. Equipped with little except the "simple mariner's compass of scientific conscience and common sense" (15), men like Friedrich Wilhelm Heinrich Alexander von Humboldt, Thomas Huxley, Alfred Russell Wallace and Ernst Haeckel (apart from Darwin himself) took to uncharted seas and territories. Such voyages threw up exciting new facts of natural history.

The prevalent science in the Victorian era was a popular science, with the foregoing voyages and expeditions drumming up enthusiasm among the masses. As Kelly Boyd and Rohan McWilliam point out,

> People at all social levels were interested in reading about new inventions and theories. Before 1900, the lay person could (up to a point) follow much of what was going on in science and the strict demarcation between professional scientist and the ordinary person did not exist in quite the same way as in the twentieth century. (253)

At times writers caustically treated the subject of popularisation of science, where true and rigorous scientific pursuits were trivialised by the dilettantes. The foolish and fatuous Mr Brooke in Eliot's *Middlemarch* is one such, and the following words uttered by him perfectly capture the degradation of science into a fad because of shallow people like him: "I went into science a great deal at one time; but I saw it would not do" (39; Bk 1, Ch. 2). Meredith's characters such as Willoughby in *The Egoist* (1879) and Sir Austin in *The Ordeal of Richard Feverel* (1859) are also examples of dilettantes without the humility and open-mindedness that seem necessary for genuine scientific interest.

Nevertheless, science's popularity was for the most part genuine enough, and its power in the Victorian period also partly stemmed from such popularity. No wonder then that science infiltrated into literature and other non-science disciplines. Many popularisers of science, such as Thomas Huxley, worked tirelessly to bring science and scientific lessons close to people, feeling that the world needed to break free from the indefensible dogmas of the past. Huxley and others often lectured to the public, including the working classes. This was his view of scientific knowledge (whose merit he was positing against that of literature): "I find myself wholly unable to admit that either nations or individuals will really advance, if their common outfit draws nothing from the stores of physical science" (Otis 6). The implications of the scientific discoveries that were swirling around were the kind that the common people could thus appreciate and share in. While preservers of the old ways resisted science's progress in bafflement and dismay, the responses of ordinary people were different and often positive. Talking about *The Principles of Geology*, an outstanding example of the popularisation of science, Irvine says: "There was some pained regret among the Tories, some dignified suffering among the clergy. Oddly enough, there was some eager enthusiasm among ordinary readers" (87).

However, it would be untrue to say that scientific findings did not cause a general upheaval that was disturbing to many people. There were many – some of them of course the Tories and the clergy that Irvine talks about – who were disquieted particularly by developments which followed Lyell's book. Some of these people were literary artists who memorably registered the sense of seismic shock that contemporary science delivered to the prevailing view of existence. While writers such as Tennyson tried to grapple with their own sense of disorientation in the face of the advancing army of science, they would probably be justified in thinking that they were also voicing more widely held sentiments. Another writer who actually was a bit of an amateur in science expressed his affront at what he regarded as the negative outcomes of scientific discoveries. John Ruskin, social activist, art critic and dabbler in science (since he was a member of the Geological Society), wanted a science where the divine and the human were not cast aside. As George Levine points out, for him "every living object has a symbolic relation to some human quality and manifests some link to the transcendent"(80). However, the material goals of the nineteenth century dislodged the human and the transcendent, and science was responsible for this, in Ruskin's view. It was science which enabled the Industrial Revolution and this phenomenon permanently blackened skies and human spirits as well. By 1884 Ruskin became so infuriated by what he called modern science's morbid belief that it could learn from death what can only be taught by life, that he resigned his Oxford professorship. Science was also bad because ultimately it was anti-religion. The testimony of Ruskin is important because he was not one of the crowd who were dismayed by the march of science and its revelations. A man endowed with genuine scientific curiosity and knowledge, he nevertheless shied away from endorsing science.

While society had already been influenced by phenomena such as the Enlightenment and the Industrial Revolution and so no longer held to completely regressive or obscurantist views of old, there was much work for science to do still. It had to challenge the prevailing theological view of human existence. According to this view, there was a divine design which oversaw everything, which conferred meaning in general, and steered everything towards Judgement Day where all wrongs would be righted. The non-geological version of the creation of the world was derived from a miraculous view of God's will and power enshrined in *Genesis* in the Bible. Everything was quick here. God said, "Let there be light, and there was light."

What was greatly unnerving about the scientific or geological version of creation was that it introduced unimaginably vast scales of time and space measurement into human consciousness. While "eternity" was a word or concept that was freely bandied around by theologians, it was something that the human mind did not have to painstakingly map or track. Actually, in the Christian scheme of things, "eternity" was a comforting myth. Unless one was talking about the eternal torment in hell, it was something that the virtuous could actually look forward to. Clerical thinkers and literary artists sketched radiant pictures of heaven. Even when earthly wrongs seemed to make existence on this earth well nigh unbearable, there was the afterlife as compensation. God had, after all, made man in His own image, and so would care for him.

Science did not respect hierarchies. Such respect was the cornerstone of the traditional, religious view of the world, especially when it came to the viewpoint of the official Anglican world. This traditional view was what at one time went by the appellation, Great Chain of Being. Humans were near the top or apex of this chain, the animals far below. Now science became more interested in the human's affinity to the monkey (and other animals) than in his difference or distance from these creatures. Scientists were as interested in the littlest of insects or animals as they were in humans.

For Darwin in particular there were no real higher and lower positions in the animal world. Darwin's essentially benign explorations still corkscrewed everything out of shape. Geology seemed to join hands with zoology to set *Genesis* at nought and annihilate man's fondest fancies. People were informed that their great ancestor was not Adam, an angelic being made from God's ribs, but a hairy ape. Sabbath was a meaningless conception because the world was formed in aeons, and not in six days with the seventh day marked for Sabbath (signifying that even God rested on that day after his labours.) As Tennyson points out memorably,

> But I should turn mine ears and hear
> The moanings of the homeless sea,
> The sound of streams that swift or slow
> Draw down Æonian hills, and sow
> The dust of continents to be; (XXXV, ll. 8–12)

There was a heartless monotony about this seemingly destructive process that chilled Victorian hearts.

Unlike many other writers and thinkers of the time, George Eliot seemed to be willing to align herself with the new scientific thinking. Having lost her early Evangelical faith, she acquired a scientific mindset through her vast readings primarily through being granted access to the famous library of Arbury Hall. It helped that the man with whom she lived out of wedlock for the better part of her life, George Henry Lewes, was also something of a scientist. Particularly in her great work *Middlemarch*, but also in her lesser works, Eliot features or mirrors some of the prominent scientific ideas of the times. One of the protagonists of the novel, Lydgate, is a medical practitioner, a scientist with a vision. There is another man with scientific pretensions, Farebrother, who is interested in old style natural history (or botany in today's parlance). He is not unlike Darwin's own father who was a collector of plant and animal specimens. However, one need not have to step into Lydgate's or Farebrother's shoes to appreciate the scientism that pervades the novel. The device of the omniscient narrator itself seems to have behind it a scientific impulse and orientation. As Diana Postlewaithe points out,

> On one hand, we find in all of George Eliot's fiction the keenly appreciative eye of the "natural historian," delineating the evocative particularities of a "singularly rich" array of human nature. On the other, those individualized characters are also richly contextualized within the reflective generalizations of an omniscient narrator "bitten with an interest in structure," a discriminating creator who identifies and delineates larger patterns of meaning. (100)

The omniscient narrator of Victorian fiction has been called a god-like figure. However, in these cases he is more observer and analyser than God. The microscope, an invention that was greatly popular in the time is an apt metaphor for the narratorial perspective that is valorised in this novel. The narrator puts human conduct, motive and follies and foibles under the microscope, as it were. Nothing escapes the narrator's eyes. In general, the realistic fiction becoming greatly popular around this time certainly privileged the minute, scientific observation of human affairs and the natural world. Eliot herself was regarded as a leading light of nineteenth-century realism. She (or rather her surrogate the omniscient narrator) observes notes and dissects, just as many scientists of the times did. The traditional categories of knowledge, heavy with the burden of spreading the affirmation of religion and spirituality, is discarded in favour of the realistic method. This realistic method or realism takes nothing for granted. It tries to do full justice to the hard, concrete facts (often the rather important trivia of domesticity) that stared one in the face. Imagination, a legacy of the Romantics, is also held in check.

The triumph of realism in the fiction of the period unquestionably points to the influence of science. Realistic fiction entailed discovering motives and causes and effects as well as verification. Things could not be just passed off as true (or left to the imagination) but pertinent facts had to be unearthed and verified through the production of evidence or testimony in the form of details which might include the seeming trivia of life. It was all about explanation, clarity, and closure. Nothing erupted from nowhere; one thing led to another with a measure of predictability or plausibility. Narrative logic or laws reflected the laws of science that formed the bedrock of life.

Of course, it has to be pointed out that even when writers incorporated scientific notions, they exercised the right to use them according to plot requirements. Even when they followed contemporary narrative patterns and conventions, it was their individual genius that finally decided how the plot would go. To say that realism (deriving from the exactitude of science and its compulsion to find material causes for everything) was the dominant mode in the age of science would not be telling the whole truth. Realism can be dull and plodding, but science had its excitement and romance with its ability to break open treasure-chests of knowledge so far hidden from human eyes. Science can be said to have lent its romance and excitement to literature. We could still call such literature realistic, if by 'realistic' we mean something that has a vital relationship to the rhythm and swing of the new world-order. When Peter Brook the psychoanalytical-structuralist critic talks about the "motor force" of narrative, he has in mind the driving energies of the nineteenth century (90). In this period "ambition" (which fuels many of the works he discusses) is a concrete, context-specific word, and not a vague universal. The Industrial Revolution is a roaring force, nourished by science and technology, and the energies of this phenomenon pass into Victorian works.

The biblical flood that forms the climax of the novel, *The Mill on the Floss,* is a kind of romantic solution to the entanglements of a narrative that had proceeded on a reliance on diurnal domestic realties. The flood does not follow naturally from what has gone before; the life of Maggie Tulliver is somewhat slow and dreary, like that of many women of the period. Miraculous transformations and quick fulfilments were not their usual lot. But the flood is sudden and catastrophic and its suddenness seems part of a different vision. There is death at the end in a way that is noble and fulfilling, investing the characters with a tragic halo. But Eliot wanted her own transcendent, overriding ambitions held in check in reality by the frustrations of being a woman to be reflected in the tragic destiny of Maggie Tulliver, and her life being cut short is an echo of that frustration or non-fulfilment. The grand ending is a good example of the way the *merely* scientific or realistic will always be modified by a writer according to her needs.

It can be argued, however, that Eliot progresses a little bit more exactly along the realistic or scientific path when she goes on to write her epic of common life, *Middlemarch* (1872). The concern that seems to be reflected in the pages of *Middlemarch* is the relation between the organism/individual and "its" environment. Apart from Eliot, writers such as Kingsley and Hardy dealt in different ways with the way the organism sought its place in the wider world, and sometimes failed. In the Darwinian scheme, while external conditions are not necessarily assigned much potency in changing a creature, everything or everyone had its/his niche or slot in the world, and if the organism could not find or adapt itself to this niche, it was headed for termination.

Such failures were an indication of the fact that Wordsworthian harmony had become untenable in the face of Darwinian discoveries about mutation and extinction.

As Terry Eagleton points out in a chapter on Charles Dickens, "As Nature comes to mean Darwinian strife rather than Wordsworthian harmony, it is less and less reliable as a norm" (147). It was also the case that Nature ceased to be the all-encompassing, all-inclusive term that it was in earlier days. "Following nature" (a popular slogan of the eighteenth century) gave way to studying nature in its multi-dimensional complexity, as also in the more rigorous business of adapting oneself to it. In the purely natural environment creatures struggled to adapt, and failed or succeeded. The failure or success, rise or fall of characters in literary narratives certainly echoed such eventualities.

While the new science edged out old-fashioned, romantic views of nature as well as religious versions of the world, and while much literary writing often showed a sense of resistance to or resentment about the triumph of science, on the whole the relationship between science and literature was a productive and mutually fortifying one. Even when writers complained about the negative aspects of science and technology, it could be said that they had at least found new subjects to talk about. That the discipline of science itself was regarded as part of literature has also been pointed out by many. Writers such as Mathew Arnold, who prided themselves on their breadth of vision and their cosmopolitanism, argued that science was also a kind of literature.

What is probably more worthy of remark is the inter-dependence of scientists and literary writers. As already indicated, many writers incorporated scientific themes or ideas into their works (this will be elaborated upon later in the chapter). Literary journals such as *Household Words* and *Blackwoods* often carried articles on science and related subjects. The literary techniques of poets and novelists also bore the influence of science. The microscopic method in *Middlemarch* is a case in point. The very relationship between the author of this novel and the man in her life provides a paradigm for the interdependence of science and literature. As Diana Postlewaithe points out, "Lewes aspired to be a 'poet in science'; Eliot, to be a 'scientific poet'. Reading George Eliot's fiction alongside George Henry Lewes's scientific writings reveal the complementary concerns of 'poet' and 'scientist' "(107–08).

More dominant and striking was the paradigm of evolution. Evolutionary narratives abounded in the Victorian period. The developmental, goal-oriented progressions of many novels of the period seemed to bear the influence of the concept of evolution with its relentlessly forward-moving thrust. To say that in the progress-oriented nineteenth century, writers emulated the linear impulse of evolution may, however, be a simplification. The significant role of the past has already been mentioned. Sometimes, as in Hardy and somewhat less seriously in the Kingsley of *The Water Babies*, such evolutionary narratives also registered the price of progress through the fates of characters or certain ways of life which were left by the wayside as being not adaptable enough to the new environment. Also, Darwinian notions of randomness militated against the earlier neatness whereby the shapeliness and regularity of the natural order as mirroring God's design was emphasised. In *Origin* we frequently come across a sense of mystification and unknowability. Such acknowledgements of the essential impenetrability of existence or of the inadequacy of human knowledge is a far cry from earlier prophecies and tendencies towards preordainments. It makes for a modern view of life which shies away from the simple wholeness of an integration of human hopes with the overarching reality and which would rather keep things somewhat open-ended.

The very title of Beer's well-known book, *Darwin's Plots,* is a pointer towards the connection or interrelationship between science and literature. One can make sense of things through discerning or making plots, and the sense of narrative that writers and scientists share is mutually beneficial. "Because of the shared discourse not only *ideas* but metaphors, myths, and narrative patterns could move rapidly and freely to and fro between scientists and non-scientists" (Beer 5).

Many of these non-scientists employing scientific themes were literary artists. Beer just a while earlier talks about the way scientists borrowed methods and ideas from literature: "Moreover, scientists themselves in their texts drew openly upon literary, historical and philosophical material as part of their arguments: Lyell, for example, uses extensively the fifteenth book of Ovid's *Metamorphosis* in his account of proto-geology" (5). After pointing out Darwin's debt to Malthus in the matter of gaining insight into the mechanism of evolutionary change, Beer says: "What has gone unremarked is that it derived also from his reading of the one book he never left behind during his expeditions from the Beagle: *The Poetical Works of John Milton*" (5).

Laura Otis also makes similar points about the interface and interdependence between literature and science: "Scientists quoted well-known poets both in their textbooks and in their articles for lay readers, and writers we now identify as primarily 'creative' explored the implications of scientific theories" (xvii). Words that she goes on to utter about the strategies of scientists reinforce what I earlier said about the popular basis of science. "The ability to express oneself articulately was essential for the communication and progress of science . . . To win the confidence of educated readers, nineteenth-century scientists made frequent references to the fiction and poetry of the day and to that of earlier generations" (xix).

While many examples can be cited about scientists adopting literary techniques or actually using works of literature as examples, the fact remains that scientists were under no compulsion to refer to or use literature. The vice versa was, however, not true. Science, backed by the Industrial Revolution and commercialism, irrevocably changed the world. There was no way that writers could ignore this changed world and its new concerns. The genre of science fiction grew up partly in response to both the power and the popularity of science. Even dystopian fiction – a branch of science fiction – made its appearance in the form of works such as *Erewhon* (1872). While this work (like most of Butler's works) and H. G. Wells's late-Victorian novels *The Time Machine* (1895) and *The War of the Worlds* (1898) were condemnatory, there were other works such as *The Water Babies* which were a little more celebratory, although there are criticisms of scientists such as Thomas Huxley and Richard Owen in this work.

There were many sciences in the period, not just evolutionary biology or geology, although these two were the ones that brought about the most far-reaching changes in human life and also seemed to have captivated people's attention and interest the most. Some of those other sciences are now labelled pseudo-sciences, such as phrenology and mesmerism. While the tenets of these sciences appear dubious today, they exercised a fascination on the minds of some of the most respectable thinkers in the Victorian period, such as Robert Browning and George Eliot. As for phrenology, one sees it appear in the role of the doctor who examines Marlow in *Heart of Darkness*, a late-Victorian work that holds up many Victorian practices up to question. The more authentic science of thermodynamics also stirred up people, with its associations of colour, motion and energy. Scottish scientist James C. Maxwell was so fascinated by its principles that he was moved to write lines such as the following:

I come from empyrean fires
From microscopic spaces,
Where molecules with fierce desires,
Shiver in hot embraces.
The atoms clash, the spectra flash, projected on the screen,
The double D, magnesian *b*,
And Thallium's living green. (Maxwell, Otis 74)

This is science *as poetry*: a good example for those who wish to emphasize imagination as a common ground between scientists and literary artists.

As in the case of evolutionary sciences, in a science like thermodynamics too analogies can be detected between various literary–social issues and the actual working of the science. Men of science with literary bents of mind as well as men and women of literature with scientific bents of mind used the prism of science to explore and evaluate problems of existence. As Laura Otis points out, both J. C. Maxwell and George Henry Lewes – the first interested in thermodynamics and the latter taking an interest in cellular biology among many other things that he cultivated an interest in – were concerned with the relationship between individual and group behaviour. Lewes, in resisting cell autonomy, "believed that consciousness and selfhood could never be associated with a single unit, only with the complex interactions in a neural or social 'web'" (xxv). As for Maxwell, he "also faced the question of individual *v.* group behaviour when he studied the movements of gas particles. Using statistical laws to describe the behaviour of matter, Maxwell found that one could not predict the movements of large groups of molecules by studying those of individual ones." Otis then goes on to make a broader comment: "In physics, sociology, and literature, the relationship between personal and collective identity remained unclear" (xxxv–vi). The point, however, is that scientific and literary studies energised each other and the explorations of issues such as individualism and societal pressures were enriched because of the reciprocity.

One last aspect that will be briefly mentioned, and that has the scope for further explorations, is the symbiosis between science and colonialism that was visible during the pre-Victorian and Victorian periods. The confidence and sense of excitement that marked the scientific scene in these periods was matched, and complemented, by similar confidence and excitement in colonial ventures. Science helped colonialism and vice versa. Many colonial administrators and army men were also avid amateur scientists. They often brought back plant and animal specimens to the mother country. Scientific investigators on the other hand, became part of colonial expeditions in foreign lands already colonised or about to be colonised. Certainly, it helped such scientists when they could travel with ease through foreign lands that hoarded exotic flora and fauna which would enable them to explore new research horizons, if those lands were under British control.

However, apart from pure scientific motives, material ambitions of exploitation of the resources of the colonies also accreted to the bedrock of scientific explorations. Talking about the ramifications of scientific expeditions in the eighteenth century under the tutelage of Joseph Banks, naturalist and sponsor of scientific expeditions, David McKay points out,

> The concentration of collectors generally in three main regions – India/Southeast Asia, the Pacific and Australasia, and the West Indies and Central America – is indicative of an important aspect of Banks's imperial philosophy. Many of these men were part of a complex network of plant exchange intended to strengthen and rationalize the economic resources of empire . . . The principal recipients in the exchange were the West Indies and the British territories in India. The principal donors were the new lands: the Pacific, Southeast Asia, China, Spanish America, and the Indian states. (47)

What was true for the eighteenth century continued to be valid for the nineteenth century and the Victorian period also. But even broader implications could be read into such scientific/colonial ventures, as McKay does: "The first task of the Banksian collectors was therefore to transcend the chaos of the lands they visited and reduce the natural world of empire to order. This work could be done only by Europeans, since it was generally agreed that science in and learning in new lands were at best obscurantist and worst nonexistent" (54). It should be apparent how such "scientific" attitudes could legitimise various colonial enterprises of dominating other people by invalidating their experience and perspectives and thus use their resources.

In the period following the Victorian age science would become a tool of dominance and destruction to a much more frightening degree. Armed with weapons of extraordinary efficiency and lethality, humankind would wreak havoc on one another in the modern period. Some see the First World War as the last battle among the colonial powers and also as the logical culmination of colonialism with its agendas of greed, cruelty, exploitation, and a no-holds-barred competiveness. As already indicated, the exploring, questing spirit of the eighteenth and nineteenth centuries had the underlying themes of domination and exploitation. In some ways, this dominating spirit gathered force and finally went out of control, leading to conflicts among the Western nations.

The dark powers of science were manifest in various military and dystopian scenarios of the nineteenth and twentieth centuries. There were also stirrings of human engineering and other instances of science running amuck which late Victorian and early-modern writers such as Samuel Butler (in *Erewhon*), Robert Louis Stevenson (*Dr Jekyll and Mr Hyde*) and H. G. Wells (in more than one work) explored and anticipated in a cautionary spirit. However, all this cannot negate the substantial achievements of science. After Darwin's discoveries in the

Victorian period, it would not have been possible to live in an illusory world of divine guidance and care. Humankind would henceforth march forward on its own.

Works Cited

Beer, Gillian. "Introduction." *The Origin of Species by Charles Darwin*. Oxford, New York: Oxford UP, 1998. vii-xxviii. Print. Oxford World's Classics.

———. *Evolutionary Narrative in Darwin, George Eliot, and Nineteenth Century Fiction*. Cambridge: Cambridge UP, 2004. Print.

Boyd, Kelly and McWilliam, Rohan. *The Victorian Studies Reader*. London and New York: Routledge, 2007. Print.

Brook, Peter. *Reading for the Plot: Design and Intention in Narrative*. New York: Alfred A. Knopf, 1984. Print.

Darwin, Charles. *The Origin of Species by Charles Darwin*. Oxford, New York: Oxford UP, 1998. Print. Oxford World's Classics.

Davis, Philip. *The Victorians. The Oxford English Literary History: Volume 8: 1830–1880*. Oxford: Oxford UP, 2002. Print.

Eagleton, Terry. *The English Novel: An Introduction*. Malden, MA: Blackwell Publishing, 2005. Indian Reprint. New Delhi: Atlantic Publishers and Distributors, 2005. Print.

Eliot, George. *Middlemarch*. Harmondsworth, Middlesex, England: Penguin Books,1983. Print. The Penguin English Library.

Gribbin, John and Michael White. *Darwin: A Life in Science*. London: Simon and Schuster, 1995. Print.

Hardy, Thomas. *Jude the Obscure*. Harmondsworth, Middlesex, England: Penguin Books,1979. Print. The Penguin English Library.

———. *The Mayor of Casterbridge*. London: Penguin Books, 2003. Print. Penguin Classics.

———. *Tess of the D'Urbervilles*. New Delhi: Oxford UP, 2005. Print. Oxford World's Classics.

Howard, Jonathan. *Darwin: A Very Short Introduction*. Oxford: Oxford UP, 1982. Print.

Huxley, Thomas. "From *Science and Culture* (1880)." *Literature and Science in the Nineteenth Century: An Anthology*. Ed. Laura Otis. Oxford: Oxford UP, 2009. 04–06. Print. Oxford World's Classics.

Irvine, William. *Apes, Angels, & Victorians: The Story of Darwin, Huxley, and Evolution*. New York: McGraw Hill Book Company, 1955. Print.

Levine, George. *Realism, Ethics and Secularism: Essays on Victorian Literature and Science*. Cambridge: Cambridge UP, 2008. Print.

Maxwell, James Clerk. "To the Chief Musician upon Nabla: A Tyndallic Ode." Laura Otis. "Introduction." *Literature and Science in the Nineteenth Century: An Anthology* . Ed. Laura Otis. Oxford: Oxford UP, 2009. 74–76. Print. Oxford World's Classics.

McKay, David. "Agents of Empire: The Banksian Collectors and Evaluation of New Lands." *Visions of Empire: Voyages, Botany, and Representations of Nature*. Eds. David Phillip Miller and Peter Hanns Reill. Cambridge: Cambridge UP, 2010. 38–57. Print.

Otis, Laura. "Introduction." *Literature and Science in the Nineteenth Century: An Anthology*. Ed. Laura Otis. Oxford: Oxford UP, 2009. xvii–xxviii. Print. Oxford World's Classics.

Postlewaithe, Diana. "George Eliot and Science." *The Cambridge Companion to George Eliot*. Ed. George Levine. Cambridge: Cambridge UP, 2001. 98–118. Print.

Tennyson, Alfred. "In Memoriam." *The Poems of Lord Tennyson*. London: J. M. Dent & Sons Ltd, 1933. Print.

THREE

The Industrial Revolution, Mercantilism, Class, and the City

As Paul Johnson points out, the Victorian economy was "bigger, faster, richer, and more encompassing than man had previously seen" (203). The phenomenon which was responsible for this magnified state of affairs was the Industrial Revolution. While this really began in the eighteenth century, it consolidated its grip on different terrains and spaces of the nation only in the nineteenth century. The identity of Great Britain underwent a steady shift over the course of the century, from being agricultural to being industrial. In the words of the historian David Thompson,

> Most Englishmen in 1815 (this was the year in which England won the Battle of Waterloo with Napoleon of France and thus is regarded as a landmark year in the history of England) still worked on the land or in trades connected with agriculture, though within the next generation most Englishmen became townsmen engaged in industry: sixteen years after Waterloo probably half the population already lived under urban conditions. (11)

However, even much later agriculture continued to provide employment to large numbers of people and by becoming mechanised and commercial, it actually became part of the narrative of industrialisation. But the agriculture vs. industry binary and the related rural vs. city opposition continued to function at an imaginative level for many people.

There were investment booms and bonanzas, and the kinetics of the market had instigated a great vertical and horizontal mobility among the populace. The policy of Free Trade encouraged by Whig and liberal governments was to a large extent responsible for such dynamism. The nation was on the move; many people were literally and metaphorically going places. Prosperity had increased manifold with the production of goods on very large scale of economies as also with the facilitation of the movements of these goods to various buyers' and sellers' markets through the railways and other transport solutions.

The railways, easily one of the most striking symbols and agents of this revolution, and a great herald of modernity, reached into remote and secluded geographical locations, and bound the country in an iron network. The hardworking Caleb Garth in the novel *Middlemarch* is excited by the new machine-driven culture in general ("the signal-shouts of the workmen, the roar of the furnace, the thunder and plash of the engine, were a sublime music to him [283; Bk 3, Ch. 24]) and also finds himself defending the railways: "Somebody told you the railroad was a bad thing. That was a lie. It may do a bit of harm here and there, to this and to that; and so does the sun in heaven. But the railway's a good thing" (604; Bk 6, Ch. 56).

A dispassionate appraisal of the Industrial Revolution (especially as the phenomenon that fired the literary imagination across two centuries) shows that it was no isolated, self-contained phenomenon, only affecting the lives of those directing making their living from it – that is, the factory owners and workers. Obviously, it had deep connections with the science of the day as various scientific inventions initiated the conditions for the great event and kept its wheels rolling. But the Industrial Revolution in England came to be much more than the child or handmaid of the scientific spirit that blossomed in the wake of the Enlightenment. It is memorable for the way it re-structured society itself, creating new classes and sharpening already existing class-divisions. In the eighteenth and nineteenth centuries, it simply pervaded the lives of the entire population apart from creating new populations in the northern cities such as Liverpool, Manchester and Birmingham. It was an unstoppable force that spread in all directions and brought vast changes into the lives of people. While England had in some ways always been an "industrial" nation, in the sense that people manufactured various articles of clothing and other items at home and in small shops, the advent and use of machine and power-based technology from the eighteenth century onwards meant that manufacture was now on a grander scale. Devices such as the steam-powered spinning-jenny invented by James Hargreaves and patented by Richard Arkwright in the latter half of the eighteenth century changed the entire scale of the spinning of cotton which became a leading nineteenth-century industry. After the increase of production, goods moved out of local and homely spaces into more distant, and impersonal spheres.

As has been pointed out often enough, two industries in particular were in the vanguard of the Industrial Revolution: cotton, mentioned above, and the metallurgical. Conditions were particularly favourable for the growth of metallurgical industries. In the words of John Merriman, "Britain was blessed with coal and iron ore deposits located near water transportation, which made it possible for raw materials to be transported to factories with relative ease" (564). Since many of the great inventors of the eighteenth century belonged to England, it is no wonder that iron and other metallurgical industries flourished. With the advent of the railways the metallurgical industries recieved a further fillip. Apart from helping in the movement of goods connected with this industry, the construction of railways also required iron and steel. As for cotton, England had a long history of textile industries. However, cotton proved to be a particularly popular commodity in the nineteenth century, winning for itself the title King Cotton. It also helped that England's imperial expansion ensured the flow from colonies such as the West Indies and India.

There were various reasons for the success of the Industrial Revolution in England. Apart from being blessed with mineral resources as also the means of quick transport of these resources in its raw and finished form, what further helped was the smooth and largely trouble-free credit system in England. Private enterprise was allowed to thrive in the banking sector, which meant that the burgeoning industries got the inflow of capital they needed. Everything seemed to be working in Britain's favour: "Its huge financial resources, vast manufacturing output and enormous coal reserves . . . made Britain a commercial and industrial titan, whose principal rivals, the United States and Germany, engaged much less in trade or traded mainly with Europe" (Darwin 9).

Apart from the understandable relationship with science, which ensured prosperity and progress on all fronts, the Industrial Revolution also had a surprising religious connection. This connection, however, tells a somewhat different story of the Industrial Revolution. Many famous works of the time often dealt with both religious matters and matters of labour relations or industrial turmoil. In many cases a man of religion also happened to be representative of some class within the industry. Some of the better-known works of literature which deal with both religion and industry are Brontë 's *Shirley,* Kingsley's *Alton Locke,* Disraeli's *Sybil* and Mrs Gaskell's novels such as *Mary Barton* and *North and South.* A reading of these works leads to an illumination of the vigorous interface between these seemingly very different and even antithetical institutions.

The Dissenting, Nonconformist sects had a great sway in the lives of the common people of the industrial North of England. The reason why the politically marginal, anti-establishment Dissenting sects such as the Quakers and the Methodists penetrated the habitations of the labouring poor was simple: the question of divine justice was momentous for people who saw little or no hope of earthy justice. These people were bogged down in morasses of back-breaking toil and restrictive and punitive laws that turned life into some kind of endless punishment. The great successes mentioned earlier in this essay made little beneficent impact on their lives. If anything, the success took a toll on *their* lives while enhancing the living conditions of the manufacturing classes. The State seemed to be smoothening the paths to the progress of this class while remaining impervious to the sufferings of the working classes. In the eyes of the working poor, the official Church of England was in league with various arms of the State. In the Preface written by Thomas Hughes to *Alton Locke* by the Christian Socialist Charles Kingsley, we are made aware of this antipathy towards the Church through the relation of an anecdote:

> In the early summer of 1848 some of those who felt with C. Kingsley that the "People's Charter" had not had fair play or courteous treatment, and that those who signed it had real wrongs to complain of, put themselves into communication with the leaders, and met and talked with them. At last it seemed that the time was come for some more public meeting, and one was called at the Cranbourn Tavern, over which Mr. Maurice presided. After the president's address several very bitter speeches followed, and a vehement attack was specially directed against the Church and the clergy. The meeting waxed warm, and seemed likely to come to no good, when Kingsley rose, folded his arms across his chest, threw his head back, and began — with the stammer which always came at first when he was much moved, but which fixed every one's attention at

> once—"I am a Church of England parson"—a long pause—and "a Chartist; . . . ." (Kingsley, Prefatory Memoir)

While people like Kingsley tried to strike a compromise and to moderate the militant edge of the Chartists by making various appeals to their better natures, resentment about the perceived role of the Church simmered and made them open to influence by the Nonconformists. The story of the Industrial Revolution thus has to accommodate the history of nineteenth-century religion too. When one considers how people always turn to the consolations of religion when daily life becomes unbearable, the connection between religion and industry is actually not all that surprising.

The Industrial Revolution was also a powerful generative force for the creation of new classes. Apart from the simple labourers or "hands", factory conditions also demanded a new army of overseers and technicians with varying levels of skills and responsibilities. Also, the Industrial Revolution was responsible for the virtual creation of "shock cities" such as Manchester, Bradford, Birmingham and Liverpool which also in its new-found complexity saw the rise of various populaces. London, although geographically distant from the North, benefited from being a mercantile hub – ferrying goods produced in the industrial cities to far corners of the globe. In the words of John Darwin,

> . . . once enacted, free trade reinforced Britain's role as the world's principal entrepot, the market-place to which the world's goods could be carried without commercial restriction. It removed any limit on the City's development as the eyes and ears of the new world economy, its banker, insurer, shipping- agent and dealer. It allowed British merchants to open commercial relations with any part of the world and offer its produce to the widest selection of buyers through the London exchanges. (59)

The vibrant prosperity of London created various trades and professions, as the above quotation indicates. One needs to only peruse some of the great city novels by Dickens such as *Bleak House* and *Little Dorrit* to appreciate the varied social mosaic that was engendered by the Industrial Revolution and developments related to it.

It should be clear, therefore, that it was largely owing to the successful spread of the Industrial Revolution that England became so powerful and prosperous. The link with rapidly progressing science on the one hand and commerce on the other hand meant that it would be a force that would require the world stage to fully come into its own. Simply put, colonialism and industrialism (and commerce) became institutions whose destinies became interlinked and even inseparable in the nineteenth century. The vision of the novelists also widened in response to such linkages, and is sometimes articulated through the viewpoints or attitudes of certain characters. In *North and South* (1855), this is what the ambitious Thornton feels and hopes about his destiny: "Far away, in the East and in the West, where his person would never be known, his name was to be regarded, and his wishes to be fulfilled, and his word pass like gold" (380; Vol.2, Ch. XXV).

There was, however, a more negative connection as well. Emigration to the colonies was sometimes seen as necessary or inevitable because of unfavourable home conditions. The sincere worker William Farren in *Shirley*, dejected on being snubbed by the factory owner Robert Moore despite making only very reasonable demands, considers emigration as an option. On the other side of the class divide, the cruel and callous aristocrat Lord Marney in *Sybil* (1845) sees emigration as a solution to rid the country of unwanted elements. Many working-class agitators were actually expelled ("transported," in the language of the day) after their participation in riotous activities. In an increasingly competitive world, with free trade or free enterprise the mantras on many people's lips, those who did not fit in or were deemed as not being able to contribute to the wealth or the welfare of the nation, were packed off to the colonies.

To the sensitive literary mind, the Industrial Revolution brought in its wake a string of destructive developments. It was felt that life in general and nature in particular were permanently transformed for the worse as the searing winds of trade and commerce scorched the face of green England. The Romantic poet William Blake had provided an early and prophetic vision of industrialism as a canker in the heart of nature as well as on the human scene with his vivid portraits of child labour. For later thinkers and writers the Industrial Revolution would be dangerous in the way it turned the scale of human values topsy-turvy and also for the sheer irreversibility of its onward march. Today's eco-critics can acknowledge a debt to the Victorian art critic John Ruskin whose religious and aesthetic sensibilities were outraged by the march of the unheeding juggernaut that was the Industrial Revolution and who sketched some of the first denunciatory images of industrialism in his writings.

Ruskin, who saw divinity in nature, perceived a defilement of nature due to industrialisation which was becoming an omnipresent and omnipotent force. This is what he says in "Modern Manufacture and Design": "that from shore to shore the whole of the island is to be set as thick with chimneys as the masts stand in the docks of Liverpool: that there shall be no meadows in it; no trees; no gardens; only a little corn grown upon the housetops . . . " (quoted in Rosenberg 223). A little later in this published lecture, he describes a stream becoming "black as ebony and thick with curdling scum" (224). What also bothered Ruskin and others was the way the success of the Industrial Revolution fuelled the increasing consumerism and profit-worshipping tendencies of the land. In religious terminology this was seen as the worship of the false god Mammon. In his famous work *Unto this Last,* he uses the expression "covetous machine" while subjecting the contemporary school of political economy to critical appraisal. As we will see, Ruskin was no voice in the wilderness, crying out against the ills of industrialism all on his own. His mourning of the desecration of nature is reflected in the lamentations of many poets while his critical dissection of Utilitarianism and political economy, with its inculcation of the calculating habit of mind found an echo in the writings of William Carlyle, Charles Dickens and others. The general culture of money would also have many detractors, from Thackeray to Lewis Carroll.

While the Industrial Revolution could be credited with stimulating social mobility of the kind mentioned in the beginning of this essay (and which was complementing other levelling or equalising tendencies in this democratic, reform-minded age), all too often the benefits of such social mobility failed to be of the kind and extent that it had the potential for. As Paul Schlicke points out, discussing the fate of the reprehensible factory owner Bounderby, "he is finally exposed as a sham, and with his discomfiture Dickens gives the lie to the Utilitarian principle that pursuit of individual fortune benefits society as a whole" (xiii). It is a rich minority that derives full advantages of industrial progress. They do not want to acknowledge their debts to the rest of society and are impatient at any attempt to curb their "freedom". "Do you give your servants reasons for your expenditure, or your economy in the use of your own money? We, the owners of capital, have a right to choose what we will do with it," says Mr Thornton, arguing against the validity of a strike by disgruntled workers in Mrs Gaskell's *North and South* (108; Vol. 1, Ch. XV). Thornton is shown as a not ungenerous man after all, but the reality was that vast numbers of the proletariat classes remained sunk in poverty because the rich manufactures grudged them enhanced pay and benefits.

Social mobility often turned into simple social dislocation. With the construction boom going on and land being needed for new factories, people could sometimes be eased out from their places of birth and age-old habitations. Also, with mass-production of goods, many old artisans who worked with their hands and homely tools lost their living and were compelled to migrate to other places in search of employment. The land became part of new equations that destabilised people's rootedness and belongingness. Enclosure systems and consolidation of large plots resulted in small plots owned by small farms becoming unsustainable. Some land was set aside or reclaimed for industry. The lives of the landless workers, always precarious, became even more vulnerable in the new dispensation. Change was strikingly for the better for some and for the worse for many others. However, to use clichéd language, it was the one constant in a period which saw rapid mutations in the conditions of life. It is as if the scenario of construction (with many houses being pulled down) that greets Michael Henchard in the beginning of *The Mayor of Casterbridge* held portents for the protagonist of another novel of his, *Tess*. In that novel, the family of Tess is uprooted and has to join moving masses of humanity going to an alien place, with the implied knowlcdgc that their places would be taken over by others.

The lot of those who found secure employment was not necessarily better. Actually, because of restrictive laws which were heavily loaded in favour of the rich employing classes, security of both career and life was a fragile thing for the working classes. Although the nineteenth-century England thrived on the dynamics of free trade, and generally prided itself on the triumph of free and liberal principles, the freedom remained the preserve of a few in real terms. After pointing out that individual workers had freedom in the matter of changing jobs and in the matter of changing places of work too, Paul Johnson points out various legal impediments of the labour market which severely restricted the actual rights of workers and often brought down the heavy hand of the law on their heads if they were perceived to be striking out on their own. The discrimination in favour of masters and against servants was almost complete: "English law gave employers the right to have workers imprisoned at hard labour for up to three months for the crime of failing or refusing to perform their labour agreements. By contrast, employers who were found to be in breach of contract with their workforce were subject only to the civil-law sanction of paying compensation" (Johnson 217).

Such criminalisation of labourers or workers was obviously a sore point and caused great resentment. The role of the master as punisher is seen in *Shirley* when Robert Moore almost *becomes* the law as he has the troublemaking preacher-agitator Moses taken into custody. David Thompson talks about "the savagery of the laws and the penalties to which the working classes were subjected" (17). The prosecutions continued late into the century. They were indicators of the fact that the industrial landscape would be in ferment throughout the Victorian period. (While labour problems have not entirely disappeared even in the twentieth and twenty-first centuries, workers now enjoy much better protection from the law.) However, to appreciate the strong feelings that made the master-servant divide such an intractable one during much of the Victorian era, one has to go back to the beginning of the century. Some of the most notable writers also responded through their writings to the developments that made the nineteenth century begin on such an ominous, stormy note.

The first decades of the nineteenth century echoed to the salvoes of the Napoleonic Wars. There were complex consequences to this devastating war, but a notable development was the fall in wages and the fall of prices of commodities with which the lives of people were concerned. Working communities were pushed to the corner by such developments; their life-conditions plummeted to new lows. In 1815 a Corn Law was passed by the parliament which stopped the import of corn to protect the British farmers who produced the item. However, while some landed interests may have benefited from this protectionist measure, there was a lot of distress among most people, as bread produced from corn was a staple item of consumption and bread becoming dear impacted everything in a negative manner. The working classes suffered particularly. The champions of free trade saw to the repeal of the Corn Law in 1846, but by then a lot of damage was done.

Although the Industrial Revolution was accompanied by a rapidly striding, progressing science which meant better medicines, better hygiene, and which in some ways ensured positive developments such as decline in mortality, in many towns, festering slums grew up at the same time. In such slums diseases such as typhus, dysentery and tuberculosis could strike lethally and frequently with basic amenities unavailable to most of the industrial proletariat. One of the most vivid and shocking descriptions of working-class life is to be found in the novel *Sybil*, a novel written interestingly enough, by a man who would go on to become one of the best-known conservative politicians of the era. Here, at first the idyllic charms of the rural town of Marney greet the eye, but harsh reality awaits the visitor:

> The contrast between the interior of the town and its external aspect was as striking as it was full of pain. Before the doors of these dwellings, and often surrounding them, ran open drains full of animal and vegetable refuse, decomposing into disease, or sometimes in their imperfect course filling foul pits or spreading into stagnant pools, while a concentrated solution of every species of dissolving filth was allowed to soak through, and thoroughly impregnate, the walls and ground adjoining. (52; Bk 2, Ch. 3)

Disraeli then goes on to describe the horribly cramped conditions in which families not only have to live but also give birth to children and rear them. The irony of his vision is that while some people live like animals in this manner, in the same nation there are certain people who live amidst splendour and gaiety. These are the lords and ladies who spend their times gossiping and enjoying various sports, balls and other upper-class recreations. Also, many of such people are indifferent, dismissive and even downright hostile regarding the needs and demands of the working populaces.

There were many others who also came up with pictures of squalor and suffering in the newly industrialised parts of the country. Kingsley offers a similar portrait of harrowing working environment towards the beginning of *Alton Locke*: "He [God]made me one, that I might learn to feel for poor wretches who sit stifled in reeking garrets and workrooms, drinking in disease with every breath,— bound in their prison-house of brick and iron, with their own funeral pall hanging over them, in that canopy of fog and poisonous smoke, from their cradle to their grave" (Ch. 1). Travellers from other lands (notable among them being revolutionary political thinker Frederick Engels who saw in the disfigured cityscape of Manchester an evidence of capitalist excess) were struck by the prosperity of the nation on the one hand, and the poverty of many in this same land, on the other. Such observers were painfully surprised by the extremely long hours that workers, many of them children and women, spent in cramped, unhealthy places. Such work-hours often began around five in the morning and ended at night, around six or seven. Factory owners, supervisors, and middlemen relentlessly squeezed these helpless people to get what labour they were capable of giving. In the absence of upper-class concern and adequate protective legislation, their victimisation was eternal and went unnoticed or unacknowledged.

While Disraeli highlights the physical misery of the industrial poor in an almost naturalistic manner, someone like Charles Dickens chooses to focus on the monotony and the deadness of spirit induced by factory life. In a novel such as *The*

Old Curiosity Shop he gives the reader a glimpse of degraded, depressing working class life:

> On every side, and as far as the eye could see into the heavy distance, tall chimneys, crowding on each other, and presenting that *endless repetition of the same dull, ugly, form, which is the horror of oppressive dreams* [emphasis mine], poured out their plague of smoke, obscured the light, and made foul the melancholy air . . . Men, women, children, wan in their looks and ragged in attire, tended the engines, fed their tributary fires, begged upon the road, or scowled half-naked from the doorless houses. (338–9; Ch. 45)

Vivid and convincing as this picture of proletarian existence is, it has to be said that in this early novel Dickens has not really integrated this vision into the main plot. One has to wait for a later work such as *Hard Times*, to appreciate how Dickens could treat the problem of the industrial lower classes in a more concentrated and coherent manner. This is his view of working class existence in *Hard Times* (1854):

> It (Coketown) had a black canal in it, and a river that ran purple with ill-smelling dyes, and vast piles of building full of windows where there was a rattling and a trembling all day long, and where the piston of the steam-engine worked monotonously up and down . . . It contained several large streets very like one another, inhabited by people equally like one another, who all went in and out at the same hours, with the same sound upon the same pavements, to do the same work, and to whom every day was the same as yesterday and to-morrow, and every year the counterpart of the last and the next. (28; Bk 1, Ch. v)

Such a view is not isolated. There are many more instances of life becoming mechanised and meaningless for most of the working population, and for children (the philosophy of utilitarianism operated negatively in both economics and education, according to Dickens).

As already mentioned, Dickens has a kinship with Ruskin. There is in both that vision of the water of life turning into a black foul stream. Where the situation of the workers is concerned also there is an affinity of viewpoint. Both writers make out the case in their own ways that workers deriving no joy from their work cannot really contribute to the good of either society or themselves. The following words by Ruskin seem to be a capping commentary on the lines from *Hard Times* just quoted: "To men surrounded by the depressing and monotonous circumstances of English manufacturing life, depend upon it, design is impossible" (quoted in Rosenberg 226). Later in the century, Hardy would pick up the theme in a different way. Tess is reduced to being a field-worker in a setting which diminishes her in all possible ways – bereft of the love of her life, she is just fighting for bare survival, and "(f)or hours nothing relieved the joyless monotony of things" (305; Ph.6, XLVI). As Alec badgers her again, she just works, "with automatic regularity" (306). All these writers were keenly alive to the fact that unlike workers and producers of the past, modern-day workers no longer could follow their own schedules and routines of work. They were in bondage to some unseen god.

Sybil, a determined and conscientious attempt to highlight the misery of the poor and the apathy and cruelty of the rich, essentially refers to the Chartist uprisings which shook and stirred the nation. The novel is set in the period 1837–44, a time when the Chartists, led by the likes of Feargus O'Connor, John Frost and William Lovett, were on the warpath. The focus keeps on oscillating between members of the aristocracy and the manufacturing classes on the one hand, and the impoverished proletariat and their various champions on the other. Disraeli, however, has more sympathy for the suffering poor than for their leaders with the exception of the protagonist's father.

The great scarcity of food among the proletariat, to whom the benefits of the Industrial Revolution seemed forever elusive, came to a head in the turbulent 40s, which was actually called the Hungry Forties. The decline in trade towards the end of the previous decade, fuelled and exacerbated by a bad harvest, led to hardships among the working population. The infamous Potato Famine of Ireland was actually not something confined to that country. A potato blight hit Europe in the mid-forties and spread to England, Scotland in 1845 and Ireland – where its impact was most devastating. Many people died in Ireland and there was also a massive exodus of desperate Irish to English shores. The immigrant Irish as well as many indigenous English comprised the impoverished and turbulent proletariat who struggled to provide daily bread to their kith and kin every day. Such widespread hunger was fertile territory for the Chartists, who could work on the resentment of vast sections of populace who felt that the upper classes were against giving them any kind of meaningful succour.

The Chartists were preceded by the Luddite movement in the beginning of the century, and this phenomenon provided the backdrop to works such as Brontë's *Shirley*. The movement derived its name from a character called General Ludd or Ned Ludd , probably a legendary character. The Luddites represented a section of workers who felt threatened by the increasingly large-scale use of machinery by manufacturers and industrialists. The machinery increased the efficiency of production but was perceived to be supplanting the workers themselves. There was also a feeling that because of exacting routines of work and the hard-driving ambitions of the owners, workers in some ways were made to become machines. As Igor Webb points out, writers such as Hazlitt, Cobbett and Ruskin "rose in outrage, and in the name of art and culture, against the proposition that progress means the transformation of the worker into a machine and the machine into a human being" (34).

The "big" machine from the world of industrialisation took on human attributes as it towered over and diminished the "small" machine, the hapless human. One such machine was the threshing machine, so memorably used by Hardy in *Tess of the D'Urbervilles* to bring home the sense that a new and impersonal age was upon the people. While the machine is in a field as an agent of productivity and efficiency, it dwarfs and outshines everyone, makes Tess bleed, and results in the pathetic destruction of many wild creatures of the field. While Hardy's work does not seem to refer to the Luddite riots in any way, it is still significant that many threshing machines were broken at a certain period in Victorian history. Thus *Tess* participates in its own way and at Hardy's chosen level, in the protest against the encroachment of industrialism into the lives of people. The ire of the working-class agitators was turned against the owners as well against the machines. They often indulged in violence, including breaking machines, attacking the homes of the factory owners and even killing people from the manufacturing or wealthy classes. So critical was the situation in *The Life of Charlotte Bronte* that Elizabeth Gaskell referred to the Luddites as possessing the "character of an insurrectionary army" (Ch.6, 71). Opposed to this "army" was the actual army; "By the summer of 1812 more troops were stationed in the northern counties to contain Luddism than Napoleon commanded against on the Iberian peninsula" (102).

The Chartists could be seen as carrying on the momentum of the Luddites, giving working-class agitation a sense of political direction and coherence that was lacking in the earlier movement. The path-breaking labour and political movement derived its name from a monster charter presented to the Parliament listing a series of demands, some of which actually went beyond the immediate requirements of the industrial poor. For instance, they wanted universal male suffrage, abolition of property qualifications for Members of Parliament, and the extension of universal education.

However, while these amplified aims would endow the movement with historical prestige, the Chartists were provoked onto the warpath by immediate issues of survival that afflicted the proletariat. Many of the working populations were incensed by the harsh New Poor Law, for instance. The Poor Law Amendment changed the terms of the original Poor Law of 1815 where local parishes helped its poor in one of the first concerted welfare gestures in the world. The New Poor Law wanted to make some discrimination between the really needy such as the old and the infirm from the healthier people, in particular male adults. Although reformist in intent, this legislation was in response to the criticism of those of the middle and upper classes who felt that they were being taxed so that good-for-nothing, habitually lazy people would keep getting undeserved financial support. Outdoor relief was discontinued for poor but able-bodied people *and* their families. They were more or less compelled to go into the workhouses where they had to work to get food and clothes.

The workhouse was actually a greatly feared place. Conditions were harsh, and the food and clothing doled out rather niggardly. Perhaps such a Spartan and punitive arrangement was to discourage those sections of the poor who were perceived to be habitually idle and taking the easy way out. The workhouse represented the harshness and inhumanity of institutional control rather than the earliest glimmerings of the welfare state. Orphans, the old, the sick and even the insane filled the workhouse. In the case of the orphans, that sense of being uncared for and even punished for being born into anonymous poverty is captured with great feeling and intensity in Dickens' *Oliver Twist* (1837–39). While this novel is not a very mature or accomplished work in terms of exploration of human nature or even plot development, it is still characteristic of one aspect of Dickens's creative imagination: his distrust of institutional goodwill and capacity when it came to ameliorating the lot of the distressed individual. This work continued to haunt the public imagination much after reforms were put in place, and little Oliver's plea for a little more food in the workhouse finds sympathetic hearers even in modern times.

Thus, the affected poor often being from the traditionally working class populations, Chartists found in this amendment grounds for grievance. They were angered by the harsh manner in which the Poor Law was enforced. There were other reasons for resentment, such as harsh punishment meted out to Chartist or working-class leaders. The movement would peter out around the middle of the century, and the chaotic scenes towards the close of *Sybil* in some ways are perhaps meant to capture or foresee the decline of the movement. The demand of the Chartists made little impression on the parliamentarians. Also, they could not garner enough support among the dominant middle-classes. However, Chartism's impact on the future was lasting. While some among the policy-makers were goaded into ameliorative action, members of the public debated the issues raised by them and writers and thinkers were energised in their creative endeavours as they wrote in response to these issues.

What is noticeable about this movement is the fact that workers felt that they shared interests which were different from those of other groups, and that they could systematically work together towards goals related to welfare of the working-class populations. In the words of John Merriman, "During the 1830s and 1840s, workers began to demand social and political reform. Proclaiming the equality of all people, the dignity of labour, and the perniciousness of unrestrained capitalism, the first socialists challenged the existing economic, social, and political order" (554). The Chartists managed to bring the simmering discontent of the masses to a boil, making them take part in stormy meetings of protest, processions, rallies and pamphlet distribution. As in the time of the Luddites, there was some violence too.

While the imagination of the poor caught fire due to the commitment and passion of the leaders, the general public was divided between sympathy and apprehension. The writings of the times often reflected this shifting stance or division. In *The Life of Charlotte Brontë* Mrs Gaskell evokes the fearful days of the Luddite riots. After reminding her readers "how cruel was the condition of numbers of labourers at the close of the great Peninsular war," she goes on to say: "They were maddened and desperate; and the country, in the opinion of many, seemed to be on the verge of a precipice, from which it was only saved by the prompt and resolute decision of a few in authority. Miss Wooler (a teacher of Charlotte Brontë) spoke of those times; of the mysterious night drillings; of thousands on lonely moors; of the muttered threats of individuals too closely pressed upon by necessity to be prudent; of the overt acts, in which the burning of Cartwright's mill took a prominent place; and these things sank into the mind of one, at least, among her hearers" (70). The burning of this mill is at the heart of Charlotte Brontë's *Shirley*, and Brontë herself is the "hearer" that Gaskell is referring to here. Gaskell's words are testimony to the deep impact that thc working-class ferment made on the genteel classes. While both *The Life* and *Shirley* deal with the Luddite unrest, considering the dates of their publications, it was clear that the authors would also have the Chartist agitations at the back of their minds.

On the face of it, many of these writers, poets and novelists alike, had a great deal of sympathy for the suffering poor. In fact, as the quotations from works such as *Sybil, Hard Times* and even *The Life* should indicate, the memorable portraits of working-class life by writers such Disraeli, Dickens, Kingsley, Brontë and Gaskell are indicative of the ability and willingness of these middle-class writers to transcend the limitations of their own classes and enter into the experiences and thought-processes of the class that was in reality far removed from theirs in terms of habits of mind and modes and manners of living.

Gaskell's novel, *Mary Barton,* has been credited with doing more to highlight the condition of the working-class poor than any number of pamphlets on the subject.

There can be found many passages in these works which show how hard these writers try to emphasise the urgency of the 'Condition of England' question. In many instances, the writers also imaginatively identify with the main proletarian protagonists. In *Hard Times*, the worker Stephen Blackpool is the moral centre of the part of the novel that deals exclusively with the industrial set-up (while in the more familial aspect, it is the girl Sissy Jupe who occupies this morally central position). He is Dickens's vision of the model working-class man: quiet, industrious, and self-effacing. No harm can come to society if there are more like him around. Interestingly, however, Dickens provides no vision of a model factory or factory-owner (unlike in *Sybil* where we see the ideal factory community of the benevolent factory-owner Mr Stafford) making Raymond Williams comment: "It is not the model factory against the satanic mill, nor is it the humanitarian experiment against selfish exploitation. It is, rather, individual persons against the system" (13). In *Shirley,* the much more slightly sketched character of William Farren plays the role of such a model worker. For a while at least, the portrayal of the sufferings of these characters seems to be an indictment of society (or "the system," in William's word) in general and the manufacturing or factory-owning class in particular. The deadening monotony of Coketown, already mentioned in this essay, clearly is reflective of the fact that the life of the industrial poor is filled with rigorous toil and attended by scant reward. Apart from niggardly remuneration, there is also the censorious attitude of the authorities which regarded any pleasure-seeking by the proletariat with suspicion. Dickens mentions the existence of many numerous religious sects, among whom are certain Evangelical ones. Notoriously anti-pleasure in any case, with regard to the working classes they seemed to have adopted a particularly oppressive, paternalistic, and regulatory role. In a note to *Hard Times,* Paul Schlicke points out: "Nineteenth-century Sabbatarian organizations repeatedly sought legislation to prevent all Sunday activities which seemed godless. Drinking hours, trade, travel, right of assembly, postal delivery, and bad concerts were among things restricted. Dickens vigorously opposed Sabbatarian attitudes throughout his career" (412–13). As Schlicke also goes on to point out, Dickens's retort to the attempt to curtail drinking habits among the poor was that drinking was not the cause, but the result of misery.

While all workers lived in the shadow of denial and deprivation the case of Stephen seems to be special. The awful Bounderby at first seems to be appreciative of Stephen's good work ethics, but turns against the worker when the latter seeks Bounderby's help in extricating himself from a terrible marriage with a drunken slattern. As his name indicates, Stephen's death is to be regarded as a kind of martyrdom – to the cause of heroic, unappreciated labour. Of course, he could also be seen as a simple victim, weighed down by too many forces: domestic travail, lack of sympathy from both owner and fellow-workers, absence of government legislation that would protect the interests of workers like him, and simple bad luck.

Bounderby's counterpart in *Shirley,* Robert Moore, is not a bad man. He is, in fact, the hero of two plots. In the romantic plot, he is the saviour of the pining, lovelorn Catherine. In the industrial plot, however, he is a stern, even oppressive figure, the kind that William Cobbett decried so indignantly. Moore deals with the sly, troublemaking Moses and the good and honest William with equal harshness. This is the narrator's remark on Moore's unyielding attitude: "by speaking kindly to William Farren, – who was a very honest man, without envy or hatred of those more happily circumstanced than himself, thinking it no hardship and no injustice to be forced to live by labour;

disposed to be honourably content if he could but get work to do, – Moore might have made a friend. It seemed wonderful how he could turn from such a man without a conciliatory or sympathizing expression" (140–41; Ch. 8).

The narrator, clearly reflecting the author's viewpoint, rues this as a missed opportunity. (Later Moore would pay for his hardness by suffering a near fatal attack by an aggrieved and demented worker.) This seems to be the consensual diagnosis of the ills of industrial relations – there is a tragic misunderstanding between man and master, with the masters to be faulted mainly for a bit of unnecessary hardness while the men are simply misguided and therefore take recourse to suicidal, violent action. When Moore tells Moses that "the persons behind you are some of them honest though misguided men" (138), he is probably reflecting a fairly widespread view. After making a quick trip to strike-hit Preston in 1854 to gather material for *Hard Times,* Dickens arrived at the assessment that "the workers' action was misguided" (Schlicke xiv). In this novel the trade unionist Slackbridge, with his false and inflated rhetoric, is the man who leads his followers astray. Charles Kingsley, another notable Victorian writer who prided himself on his sympathetic stance vis-à-vis the struggling poor, felt that trade unionists or demagogues were turning the workers against the upper classes, many of whom were actually benefactors of the industrial poor.

As the above instances indicate, most of these middle-class writers display a conservative streak while dealing with these issues. It is as if they understand the cause of the protest and resistance, but cannot bring themselves to endorse the methods adopted by the protesters. The explicitly political agenda of the workers disquiets them. The conservatism of the writers takes many forms. In different ways, they mock or undermine the stance of the more implacable of the movement leaders. It is almost as if the hidden self-seeking or general misanthropy is what actually prompts certain men to become leaders. The portrait of men such as Moses and Slackbridge seem to reveal a deep-seated fear of being swamped by hordes of militant workers whose passions are ignited by political rhetoric. Probably the writers along with their middle-class and upper-class readers felt that the workers had the ultimate goal of radically readjusting hierarchies and class-relations: that is, seize political power. In her biography of Brontë, Gaskell refers to the Luddites "as almost to assume the character of an insurrectionary army" because of their sheer numerous strength (*The Life of Charlotte Bronte* 71).

They also seem to display admiration for certain representatives of the manufacturing or ruling classes despite the latter's harshness towards the demands of the working classes many of which demands are seen as quite legitimate. Such admiration may seem quite reactionary from the modern perspective. It is as if such men may not be very pleasant but are necessary to maintain order and prevent things from getting out of hand. In real life such a one was William Cartwright whose mill-burning at Rawfolds was a famous event of the times. While the man is transformed into Robert Moore in *Shirley*, Gaskell has several references to him as she talks about the turbulent times in the biography of Charlotte Brontë partly to account for the inspiration behind *Shirley*. There is another man named Robertson who seems to be the model for the unrelenting, fighting clergyman Helstone. About Cartwright, Mrs Gaskell says that he was a "very remarkable man" (70). About the vicar Mr Robertson who is also active in his resistance to the Luddites, Mrs Gaskell's words are even more admiring: "He was loyal in every fibre to Church and king; and would have proudly laid down his life, any day, for what he believed to be right and true" (72). Gaskell does go on to say, however, that he was a man of "imperial will," because of which his name has not gone down well in history.

While Charlotte Brontë has nothing good to say about the anti-worker, anti-woman Rector Helstone, about Moore her attitude is more divided. Initially he is seen as a typically ungenerous, unfeeling employer. The incident with Farren reinforces this feeling. But gradually he is seen as an essentially good, even generous man. In his mill no child is struck (there were many child labourers in the mills and factories of England, many of whom were brutally treated). Finally, so much of the readers' goodwill is enlisted for him that he is the fit hero of the romantic plot as well. But it is not just Moore who is made the representative of the owner-class. The eponymous heroine Shirley Keeldar, never harsh to the poor as Moore is, shows a stern side to her character when she confronts the issue of the riotous behaviour of the agitators. As she says, "At present I am no patrician, nor do I regard the poor round me as plebeians; but if once they violently wrong me or mine, and then presume to dictate to us, I shall quite forget pity for their wretchedness and respect for their poverty, in scorn for their ignorance and wrath at their insolence." (269; 14). The view here is curiously "paternalistic." The workers are like children – if they step out of line, they must be punished. Like children they don't know what is good for them and they must rely on the benevolent guidance of the ruling classes. There also seems to be a strange closing of ranks. The only thing is, the closing of ranks is directed at the industrial poor. It seems as the ruling aristocracy, the industrialists, and the middle classes must form some kind of an alliance against the working classes. Despite nominally belonging to the middle-classes, the Brontës knew poverty in their own ways but they would probably feel that temperamentally they were akin to the upper-classes rather than the lower classes.

Notwithstanding the analogy between misguided workers and children, it must be reiterated that the writers share a deep fear of the poor with the rest of their countrymen and countrywomen. Such a fear of the angry poor probably existed at least since the Peasant Revolution of 1381, although in the nineteenth century fear was tinged with some compassionate understanding. Carlyle, great prophetic voice of the times and author of books such as *The French Revolution* and *Past and Present* which deal with the upsurges of discontented masses, writes this in *Chartism* : "Revolt, sullen revengeful humour of revolt against the upper classes, decreasing respect for what their temporal superiors command, decreasing faith for what their spiritual superiors teach, is more and more the universal spirit of the lower classes ... Has not broad Europe heard the question put, and answered, in the great scale; has not a FRENCH REVOLUTION been?" (34; Ch. 5). Carlylean fears about a French Revolution occurring on British soil are echoed in many of the works of the period, including some of the ones we have discussed. In *Sybil,* the character Lady Marney sounds the alarm bell by announcing to her son Egremont "that a revolution was inevitable, that all property would be instantly confiscated, the poor deluded king led to the block or sent over to Hanover at the best, and the whole of the nobility and principal gentry, and everyone who possessed anything, guillotined without remorse" (32; Bk 1, Ch. 5).

There are many portraits of raging mobs in Victorian literature, perhaps the most notable one being the bloodthirsty French Republicans in Dickens's *A Tale of Two Cities,* the author borrowing much knowledge of the event from Carlyle's book on the subject. Dickens also depicts the destructive ferocity of mobs in the much lesser known *Barnaby Rudge* (1841), a novel about the anti-Catholic riots of the end of the eighteenth century led by the violent and eccentric George Gordon. While these works maybe about non-contemporary historical events, the double vision of the Victorians ensures that the novels can be about different events at the same time. Just as *Shirley* may be about the Luddites, plot-wise, but could also be a comment on or interrogation of the methods of the Chartists, the novels of Dickens may be about the specific events mentioned above but could also reflect general fears about the swarming poor. It was the industrial Revolution that on the one hand increased the number of these poor or worsened their living conditions on the one hand, and on the other hand, instigated these poor into organising themselves into militant bands who struck terror into the people, including the writers. Dickens's *A Tale of Two Cities* is one work which may have an underlying thesis of urgency and anxiety about home conditions although it may ostensibly be dealing with the French Revolution. Revolutionary insurrections breaking out all over Europe would have sharpened fears and anxieties.

Many of these writers tried to make the point that unless matters were mended, trouble would be upon everyone. Behind the sympathy and humanism of writers such as Dickens and Disraeli lurked a fear of the mob. This reflects not only upper-class apprehensions in the novel, but also perhaps the middle-class paranoia of the writers. To the working classes, their message was to show restraint. Writers such as Disraeli, Carlyle and Kingsley, despite being of different temperaments and political and religious allegiances, felt secure in the rightness of aristocratic or upper-class leadership. Clearly, they did not trust the mob to be the best judges of their own welfare. Carlyle could be speaking for many others like him when he says in *Chartism*: "The relation of the taught to their teacher, of the loyal subject to his guiding king, is, under one shape or another, the vital element of human society" (44; Ch. VI).

Dickens was no champion of royal or aristocratic leadership, but he did not trust the trade-unionists either. When he visited Preston, the site of the industrial strike which forms the backdrop to *Hard Times*, he seemed sympathetic enough to the workers' cause. But in the novel his sympathies narrow down to intensely depicting the plight of the individual worker

Stephen Blackpool who is ostracised by his fellow-workers. The real working-class movement is denied legitimacy as it is led by the malicious, manipulative Slackbridge. It is not surprising that in an article in an 1851 issue of his magazine, *Household Words,* Dickens urged striking engine drivers and firemen of the Northwestern Railways to discontinue with their strike.

The mill owner William Rathbone Greg, after expressing some sympathy with the industrial poor, says this about trade union leaders: "Those are no true friends to the labourers or the artisan who would persuade him that the neglected duties are all on the part of his employer, and the denied or forgotten rights all on his own" (Gaskell, *North and South*, 466). He seems to be echoing Dickens's sentiments about Slackbridge as also Robert Moore's about the strike-leaders in *Shirley*. All such comments may reflect a collective feeling that today's working-class crowds may turn into tomorrow's revolutionary mobs, if they are goaded on by their leaders with their incendiary rhetoric and hidden agendas.

Frederick Engels, who along with his compatriot Karl Marx, deeply studied English working-class conditions, had his own warning to make, also invoking the French Revolution: "Hence also the deep wrath of the whole working-class, from Glasgow to London, against the rich, by whom they are systematically plundered and mercilessly left to their fate, a time almost within the power of man to predict, must break out into a Revolution in comparison with which the French Revolution, and the year 1794 [the year of the Reign of Terror], will prove to have been child's play" ("Introduction"). Unlike the English writers with their middle-class, safety-seeking sensibility, Engels was not afraid of revolutionary mobs. Fortunately for the upper-class people of England, his prophecy was not fulfilled.

Certain works, not obviously Condition-of-England or industrial in nature as *Sybil, Shirley* or *Hard Times* are, still seem to offer telling insights into the way industrialism or the

Industrial Revolution bore down on people. Tess has already been mentioned in this context. While Charlotte Brontë deals quite exclusively with the subject of industrial unrest in *Shirley*, her sister Emily Bronte's *Wuthering Heights* is preoccupied with other concerns. However, here too the Industrial Revolution seems to have a role. The chief protagonist of the novel, Heathcliff, is found on the streets of Liverpool, that burgeoning town in the heart of England's industrial North. Heathcliff could be one of the many orphans who were abandoned by parents who found themselves in a state of destitution or vagrancy on the streets of an alien city. While in the novel itself Heathcliff is conjectured to be a gypsy what with its black hair and strange tongue, Terry Eagleton offers the interesting, speculative interpretation that he may actually be Irish. (Earlier in this essay we have already pointed out that the famine forced many Irish to flee their motherland.) He also provides a wider interpretive frame to evaluate the work in terms of social history and emergent class equations:

> By 1847, around three hundred thousand of those Irish emigrants had washed up in the port of Liverpool. One London journal portrayed them, and their famished children in particular, as looking like starving scarecrows dressed in rags with an animal growth of black hair obscuring their features. Two years earlier, Branwell Brontë had himself taken a trip to Liverpool, where he might well have witnessed such scenes. (124)

The Brontës were members of the genteel classes, but it is noteworthy that their father was an Irishman who had come seeking his fortunes to England.

In one sense Disraeli was right when he said that England was a nation divided into two classes. But these two classes were also sub-divided into many more classes. Class divisions, a consciousness of the class that one belongs to and perhaps is trying to get out of, and related matters of money, property, status and career-switches form the staple of many works of Victorian literature. While many of these issues are affected by the Industrial Revolution, at times they seem to acquire a certain independence of their own. The Industrial Revolution certainly opened up the possibility for unimaginable prosperity and class transformations for other peoples if not for the working classes themselves. A dominant literary form, the bildungsroman, ostensibly dealt with the question of moral growth and maturity in keeping with the general didacticism of the age. However, the material issues of survival and improvement which underlie working class narratives also inform such bildungsromane.

The prosperity and the transformation was often made possible, or seen as possible, through migration to the cities. London in particular was an alluring destination then, as it continues to be now. While the city is one of the first mileposts of human civilisation and predates the Industrial Revolution by several centuries, the city as we know it came into its own in the eighteenth and nineteenth centuries. The populations of these towns and cities in England grew immensely over this period. In the first decades of the nineteenth century cities such as Liverpool, Birmingham and Manchester grew two times and more. As already stated, the northern industrial cities were virtually created by the Industrial Revolution, while London grew to eminence because of it. Becoming the ferrying point and hub for inflowing and outflowing goods and merchandise of various kinds, London became a world city. In becoming a complex, crowded place of perils and possibilities, London inevitably stretched the imagination of writers as various as Wordsworth and Dickens. It also struck outside visitors with awe because of its sheer size. Talking about the French critic Hippolyte Taine travelling to London, Andrew Sanders has this to say: "Taine, in common with many other visitors from abroad, could not get over the physical size of London, the greatest and most populous city of the nineteenth century. London was unprecedented. Once in its centre the encroaching city seemed to be inescapable" (114). Sanders goes on to say that "Victorian London seemed somewhat less daunting to native Londoners and to seasoned British observers."

While not quite daunted, people certainly seemed fascinated by London. In many of the works we have discussed, there are glimpses of London or London life even when the narratives are not mainly concerned with metropolitan existence and when their actions often take place in locales far from London. Elizabeth Gaskell uses rather exotic metaphors to conjure London in the mind's eye when she describes a possible career move for Patrick Branwell in her biography of Charlotte: "I dare say, he longed and yearned to follow this path, principally because it would lead him to that mysterious London – that Babylon the great – which seems to have filled the imaginations and haunted the minds of all the younger members of this recluse family" (*The Life of Charlotte Bronte* 8, Ch. 7). *Sylvia's Lovers*, which has as its setting a really remote whaling-port in the north, also provides a glimpse of London, as one character thinks about a rival character seemingly being rewarded with a business trip to a far place, although he does not know that the end-point is London: "He did not yet know of the culminating point – of Philip's proposed journey to London, that great city of London, which, from its very inaccessibility fifty years ago, loomed so magnificent through the mist of men's imagination. It is not to be denied that Philip felt exultant at the mere fact of going to London" (202; Ch. XVII). In *North and South* we are told that "London life is too whirling and full to admit of even an hour of that deep silence of feeling which the friends of Job showed"(54; Vol. 1, Ch. VI). In Disraeli's *Sybil*, the eponymous heroine in her brief sojourn in London makes an even more negative assessment of the city: "'Tis a great prison" (234; Bk 4, Ch. 6).

In the same novel there are pertinent lines uttered by a character testifying to the materialistic, mercenary principles of the city which leads to competition and alienation among human beings:

> A density of population implies a severer struggle for existence, and a consequent repulsion of elements brought into too close contact. In great cities men are brought by the desire of gain. They are not in a state of cooperation, but of isolation, as to the making of fortunes; and for all the rest they are careless of neighbours! (65; Bk 2, Ch.5)

The city is the place for money which displaces human considerations. When human beings come together or interact, they are indeed "brought together by gain." Unlike in the countryside where wealth is sometimes passive and invisible, remaining locked up in landed properties, in the city money is active and visible, flowing from various sources and to various destinations. Pip in *Great Expectations* shifts to the city primarily to acquire fine manners, but his dreams are nourished by money that flows from a mysterious source. In short, he is nothing without the money that props up his existence and the money that he keeps on spending regularly in his "gentlemanly" pursuits. He also finds that money plays a very definitive and dominant role in the lives of the people, both good and bad.

Money and class could sometimes be complementary issues, but could also be antithetical. The attitudes to money and class bring to the fore many contradictions of the age. To have money was good, but to seem to be *wanting* money was degrading. A gentleman could not be a gentleman without ample money to throw around, but he could not soil his hand by handling it in public or by working hard for it. In *Middlemarch* young Fred is desperate for money almost until the end of the narrative. However, "he held himself to be a gentleman at heart, and did not like courting an old fellow [Mr Featherstone] for money" (163; Bk 1, Ch. 14). While class-consciousness of the sort displayed by Fred could become manifest in villages and provincial places such as Middlemarch, the city provided many more shades and gradations of class. It is the city that displays class-hierarchies, the co-existence of different classes, the possibility of moving from one class to another, and the growth of new classes. Some of these classes virtually created in the city-context are law stationers and law writers, bankers, insurance and shipping managers and clerks, solicitors, sanitary inspectors, engineers, inventors, shop-owners and various other kinds of entrepreneurs, journalists, detectives, bureaucrats, moneylenders, bohemian artists or artist-types, and charity organisers. It is the clash or coming together in various ways in city spaces of these exploding diversities of classes that stimulated and shaped the creative imagination of writers such as Dickens.

While the sheer diversity of lifestyles and existence of many classes is what characterises London life, in some ways the streets belonged to the poor because simply there were so many of them. The grand "arrival" of London as a world city has this fact to reckon with, and the lives of the poor function as a subversive counter-narrative to the success stories of many who made it good through the expansions and exploitations of the potentials of urbanisation. Just as the success was starkly visible in the way people paraded their wealth in public spaces, and in the striking splendour of many houses of business and private mansions built during the period, the downsize of that success was manifest in the squalor and the filth of the 'underlife' of the forgotten or unacknowledged poor which often spilled out into those same streets. The journalist Henry Mayhew memorably captures poor lives in all their degradations in his *London Labour and the London Poor* (1851). While the work is factual and is based on the numerous interviews he took of poor people such as beggars, prostitutes, rat-catchers and costermongers,

Mayhew brought to bear a creative imagination to bear on his investigations into the seamier side of life. His stories and interviews indeed match Dickens's accounts of street life (in the latter's novels and journalistic works) in their creative energy.

The issue of class, fuelled by the Industrial Revolution and related mercantile developments, and redefined and complicated in cities such as London, was to a very large extent a matter of perception and perspective. Kelly Boyd comments that "class became less an objective reality than a story that people told about themselves to make sense of the social order (Boyd and McWilliam 28). This statement is typical of today's critical climate where representations and discursive formations are privileged. That is, how people talk about certain things rather than the so-called reality or "essence" of the thing is what is regarded as important. However, though the perceptions and consciousnesses of people reflected or embedded in various representations or narratives is important enough, the concrete reality of certain class situations in Victorian England is also undeniable. This is particularly so because the emergence of new classes re-shaped and re-configured class demarcations and class alignments. While the landed aristocracy retained prestige and privileges, and also in some measure re-invented itself by shrewdly investing its rents and other incomes in business ventures and also by forming marriage alliances with the rising merchant classes, there were readjustments lower down the social scale too. Such readjustments and sharp rise and fall patterns in the fortunes of people disturbed the simple classification of society into upper, middle and lower class, or even the simple rich–poor binary.

Apart from the existence of numerous intermediate class-gradations between the upper and lower ends of the spectrum, the volatility of the market and the economic landscape in general ensured the ascent and descent of people from class to class. The ravages of different cycles of trade and agricultural depression throughout the century meant the creation of sub-classes – for instance, the respectable poor becoming paupers, thieves and vagrants. Even among the well-to-do classes – those who had broken into the upper-classes through business opportunism, hard work and luck – abrupt diminution of status was an ever-present, dire prospect. The Railway Mania of the 1840s, where people were encouraged to invest in railways stocks and bonds, meant to finance costs of the rapidly spreading railway networks, is a case in point. Sheer bad planning, lack of foresight and many forms of sharp practices meant that the values of such stocks and shares rose dramatically and also fell dramatically. Such fraudulent practices, whereby the promise of great rewards are somewhat dishonestly dangled before a gullible populace, finds place in novels of the period such as Charles Reade's *Hard Cash,* Trollope's *The Way We Live Now,* and Dickens's *Little Dorrit.* The last-named work is also one of Dickens's more class-conscious novels. We see here characters such as Mrs Merdle and Mrs Gowan displaying or asserting their class-superiority through parodic exaggeration. A financial scandal and collapse of funds not dissimilar to the Railway Mania sees the ruin of many people. The most dramatic fall or descent, however, is that of Mr Merdle, the husband of the above-mentioned Mrs Merdle. Merdle is a man of obscure origins who rises in society through successful financial speculations and perhaps through his marriage, and who is worshipped by all and sundry. But after the scandal in which he is embroiled is exposed and he is ruined, he is regarded as just a common thief. He finally commits suicide, disowned by his wife, among others.

While many of these rise and fall phenomena have as the epicentres the city of London, the smaller towns and the countryside also witnesses up-and-down narratives linked to economical developments. Thomas Hardy explores the drama of class-related rise and fall in his country-based novels. In *Return of the Native* Clym Yeobright is a diamond merchant in Paris who returns to his village with the idealistic aspiration of being a teacher. At the end he is reduced to being a lowly furze-cutter. In *The Mayor of Casterbridge*, Hardy's exploration of this theme of rise and fall or movement from a higher class to a lower class (and vice versa) is acuter and profounder and has a sociological dimension. Michael Henchard starts his life as a hay-trusser but becomes a mayor through his talent and perseverance, but then is reduced to vagrancy after a series of mistakes and mishaps. Unlike the swindler Merdle Henchard is not really to blame, or at least, there are extenuating circumstances in his case. He is not adaptive enough to new technology as his rival Donald Farfrae is. Also, Henchard's downfall seems to reflect the agricultural depression of the 1870s. In his tragedies Hardy seems to be making a creative compromise between his antiquarian interest in *classicism* and his modern interest in *class*. Henchard and Tess are both instances of "how the mighty have fallen," an Aristotelian phrase used by a character in *Tess of the D'Urbervilles*. Tess is descended from the nobility, but is now just a humble country-maiden, reduced to drudging in fields and farms for survival.

More than most historical phenomena, the Industrial Revolution is responsible for linking the lives of the people together. Inventions such as the railways and the telegraph are only the most obvious agencies of interlinking lives. Writers often show how in a "modern" world, commercial crises can abruptly impact people's lives. In literary terms, this often means the linking of romance plots to other plots such as war, imperialism and commercial speculations. In *Vanity Fair*, in a single sentence Thackeray links the arrival of Napoleon at Cannes to a fall in British funds and subsequently to the financial ruin of John Sedley and thus also to the marriage prospects of his daughter. In the industrial novels the rich may be mentally and physically distant from the poor, but the writers try to show the impossibility and undesirability of such distancing. Connections can also be made between the lives of rural folk leading seemingly isolated lives and the many city-bred phenomena involving scientific inventions and financial wheeling and dealing. Responsible for making Britain a world power, the Industrial Revolution however also brought out the most exploitative and self-seeking tendencies of people. This ironically ushered in newer forms of misery to very large chunks of the population, and many writers of the period tried to jog the conscience of the nation regarding these new unfortunates in their often limited, middle-class ways.

Works Cited

Boyd, Kelly and Rohan McWilliam. "Introduction." *The Victorian Studies Reader.* London and New York: Routledge, 2007. 1–47. Print.

Carlyle, Thomas. *Chartism.* New York: John B. Alden, Publisher, 1885. Print.

Darwin, John. *The Empire Project: The Rise and Fall of the British World-System 1830–1970.* Cambridge: Cambridge UP, 2009. Print.

Dickens, Charles. *The Old Curiosity Shop.* Oxford: Oxford UP, 1998. Print. Oxford World's Classics.

———. Hard *Times.* Oxford: Oxford UP, 1989. Print. Oxford World's Classics.

Disraeli, Benjamin. *Sybil OR The Two Nations.* Oxford: Oxford UP, 2008. Print. Oxford World's Classics.

Eagleton, Terry. *The English Novel: An Introduction.* Malden, MA: Blackwell Publishing, 2005. Print. Indian Reprint, Distributor: Atlantic Publishers & Distributors.

Engels, Frederich. *The Condition of the Working Class in England in 1844.* Project Gutenberg e-Book. Web. 1 April 2016. <www.gutenberg.org/ebooks>.

Gaskell, Elizabeth. *North and South.* New York: W. W. Norton, 2005. Print. A Norton Critical Edition.

———. The *Life of Charlotte Brontë.* London and Melbourne: J. M. Dent, 1984. Print. Everyman's Library.

Greg, William Rathbone. "The Claims of Labour." *North and South.* Contexts 1850–1900. Ed. Alan Shelston. New York: W. W. Norton, 2005. 462–69. Print. A Norton Critical Edition.

Hall, Catherine. Ed. *Cultures of Empire: Colonizers in Britain and the Empire in the Nineteenth and Twentieth Centuries: A Reader.* Manchester: Manchester UP, 2000. Print.

Hardy, Thomas. *Tess of the D'Urbervilles.* New Delhi: Oxford UP, 2005. Print. Oxford World's Classics.

Hughes, Thomas. "Prefatory Memoir" to *Alton Locke* by Charles Kingsley. Project Gutenberg e-book. Web. 3 May 2016. <www.gutenberg.org/ebooks>.

Johnson, Paul. "Market Disciplines." *Liberty and Authority in Victorian Britain.* Ed. Peter Mandler. Oxford: Oxford UP, 2006. 203–23. Print.

Kingsley, Charles. *Alton Locke, Tailor and Poet: An Autobiography.* Project Gutenberg e-book. Web. 10 May 2016. <www.gutenberg.org/ebooks>.

Merriman, John. *A History of Modern Europe: From the Renaissance to the Present.* New York: W. W. Norton, 2004. Print.

Ruskin, John. *The Genius of John Ruskin: Selections from His Writings.* Ed. John D. Rosenberg. London: George Allen & Unwin, 1963. Print.

Sanders, Andrew. *Charles Dickens: Authors in Context.* Oxford: Oxford UP, 2009. Print. Oxford World's Classics.

Schlicke, Paul. "Introduction." *Hard Times.* Oxford: Oxford UP, 1989. Print. Oxford World's Classics.

Thompson, David. *England in the Nineteenth Century 1815–1914.* Harmondsworth, Middlesex, England: Penguin Books, 1977. Print.

Stoler, Ann Laura. "Cultivating Bourgeois Bodies and Racial Selves." Hall. 87–119.

Webb, Igor. *From Custom to Capital: The English Novel and the Industrial Revolution.* Ithaca and London: Cornell UP, 1981. Print.

William, Raymond. "The Industrial Novels: *Hard Times.*" *Culture and Society 1780–1950.* Chatto and Windus: The Hogarth Press, 1958. Rpt. in *Modern Critical Interpretations: Charles Dickens's* "Hard Times". Ed. Harold Bloom. Delhi: Worldview Publications, 2003. Print.

FOUR

Empire and Race in Victorian England

If the nineteenth century was *the Age of Empire* (title of a book by the distinguished Marxist historian Eric Hobsbawm), it was also very largely the Age of the *British* Empire. This empire had long arms, reaching into parts that were considered very remote from the perspective of Western comfort zones. In 1840, Britain ruled about a quarter of the world's entire population. There were many things that worked in Britain's favour in its drive to become a world power. Old imperial behemoths such as the Spanish empire had collapsed. While another ancient and ambitious foe France continued to spar with Britain, and while new rivals for international supremacy such as Germany and America had sprung up, there was little doubt that the island nation had the advantage. After the decisive British victories in the Napoleonic wars, France was not quite the same force at least in relation to England. Germany and America did not have England's traditional advantages such as well-established colonial bureaucracies or familiarity with distant markets and colonies of the world.

Of course, the nineteenth century, and even the Victorian period is long and varied. If we look at the imperial calendar, we will see many ups and downs: narratives of progress followed by and even accompanied by tales of setbacks and regression. The nation was also not always unified in its outlook towards Victorian imperialism or colonialism, although it is remarkable how many authors known for their outspoken condemnation of injustice at home seemed willing to overlook injustice abroad in their endorsement of British (or White) superiority and right to rule over others. Among them were not only the abrasive and loud apologist of imperialism, Lord Macaulay, but also the humanitarian or radical-spirited Dickens, J. S. Mill, and Anthony Trollope.

British power, which had been reaching out beyond near and familiar horizons since the sixteenth century at least, had a tremendous boost from political and scientific developments in the eighteenth century. Its powers also seemed pretty much unchecked through the nineteenth century. The wars with the Americans may have been setbacks, but there was compensation in the form of economic understanding with the new nation especially over the import of cotton to England. Other international developments, such as the defeat of China in the Opium Wars, and the squabbling among Indian rulers who were often friendlier to the nation ruled by Victoria than to one another, also helped in the entrenchment of the British in lands and waters far away from their own shores.

As British colonial power bloomed and spread in different directions, different narratives of the empire emerged. There were the narratives of the grander, showcase aspects: the way that Great Britain ruled the waves by identifying and often monopolising profitable sea-trade routes; the exploits of brave, marauding explorers and soldiers of fortunes such as Cecil Rhodes in Africa and Robert Clive in India; the fruits and fallouts of the Industrial Revolution that enabled the British to plant steel rails and other means of transport and communication in newly-invaded nations; the growth of London as a hub of mercantile activities of an international nature; and the successes of its Evangelical and Baptist missions abroad which ensured the neutralisation of some hostile native populations in lands where the British harboured imperial ambitions.

However, the story of empire would also have to find a place for the humble emigrant. An emigrant such as the honest Farren in *Shirley* almost felt that it was better to go abroad than be ruled by masters such as Robert Moore. Where would he go? To the various colonies in Asia and Africa or the outposts which would soon become colonies or "settler nations" such as Canada, Australia or New Zealand due to significant British footfall. Of course, the largest emigration was in the direction of the former colony that would become the United States of America.

While the story of the British empire has its dark underbelly (memorably exposed at the century's end by the Polish expatriate writer Joseph Conrad in *Heart of Darkness*), we will first consider the factors that fuelled England's success and made the Age of Empire an affair to remember with pride for generations of Englishmen. Without looking at such "positives" it will be not possible to account for many flag-waving moments in the literature of the period. And to do this we need to carry on the story of the Industrial Revolution and related commercial matters touched on a previous chapter for a while longer.

England's economy was booming in the Victorian period due to the spectacular success of the Industrial Revolution. Eric Hobsbawm, while centralising the place of the Industrial Revolution in the march of European imperialism, has this to say: "The history begins with the decisive double breakthrough of the first Industrial Revolution in Britain, which established the limitless capacity of the productive system pioneered by capitalism for economic growth and global penetration" (9). However, to realise its economic potential and to attain international pre-eminence the nation needed to connect with the rest of the wide world. What was true for the nation was true for the individual too, as the enterprising and ambitious Thornton realises in *North and South*.

England had always been a maritime power and this fact was now helpful in that import or export of goods of various kinds would flow along that best of pathways: the oceans of the world. England's geopolitical triumphs began before Victoria ascended the throne in 1837 as she had imposed herself on the high seas and the trade routes through naval battles and trade manoeuvres much earlier. By sailing the oceans she had acquired rich plantations in the West Indies that ensured the domestic prosperity of people like the Bertrams in Austen's *Mansfield Park* (1814). When the colonial situation in the West Indies became unfavourable after the ban on the slave trade and other factors, there were compensatory acquisitions or consolidations of colonial spaces elsewhere, notably in India. While the English imposed themselves culturally, religiously and politically on far-flung places of the world, the primary reason for their domination of the world stage in the nineteenth century was perhaps commercial. While it is true that the nation met with opposition from traditional or new rivals for such domination, in the largely war-free Victorian era (if we exclude the Crimean War in mid-century with Russia in which Britain came out on top despite some setbacks) large military conflicts did not drain its resources much. The Napoleonic wars of the early nineteenth century did survive in collective memory and resonated in works as diverse as *Sylvia's Lovers* and *Vanity Fair*. And devastating cataclysm ensuing from conflicting colonial ambitions lay in the future, in the form of the First World War.

The term "imperialism", despite its old legacy and association with pomp and vanished grandeur, is for Eric Hobsbawm a modern phenomenon, stretching from the 1880s to 1914 when the First World War began. It was also primarily economic and industrial. Hobsbawm contests older historians "who tended to deny any specific connection between the imperialism of the late nineteenth and twentieth centuries" (61). Earlier in the work he had already made this comment: "Change was the name of the nineteenth century: change in terms of, and to suit the purposes of, the dynamic regions along the shores of the Northern Atlantic seas which were at this time the core of world capitalism" (26).

The changes acquired a galloping character as the century progressed justifying Hobsbawm's fixation of the chronological limits for "imperialism." (Many would call it late imperialism.) Also, in this late phase, there were more formal annexations of regions which were inhabited by others but over which the British strutted and flaunted their powers. However, the changes were in evidence much earlier and those earlier changes could be said to anticipate and prepare for the later changes. One notable aspect in all this dynamism was that the military and the mercantile were intertwined. British military might supported traders in their penetrative and expansionist forays. The relationship was indeed so close that there was a blurring of the boundary, when we consider the fortunes of the East India Company. This trading company that was first granted trading rights swelled up to become a kind of superstate. Some of its commercial officials were actually warriors as much as they were traders and accountants: another very striking nexus between the military and the commercial is seen in the Indian colonial context when the British army actually employed native Indian troops for its wars in different parts of the world: "an increasingly central role was assigned to India in the expanding British empire, particularly in providing and paying for the soldiers needed to secure imperial objectives. British and Indian soldiers fought in many parts of Asia, Africa and even Europe for these ends, *their costs borne for the most part by India's agricultural producers*; and its sons, especially those of the Punjab, supplied most of the soldiery" (emphasis mine) (Stein 242).

Many instances of how trading and military interests converged while furthering the cause of empire may be found. The business of empire being primarily *business*, armed might, however, had to play a secondary or auxiliary supportive role. Also empire expansion was no longer a state enterprise. That is to say, it was not just a question of policy decisions taken at the highest levels and then clear and coherent implementations of those policies through institutions such as colonial police, the army and the bureaucracy. A whole host of individual players and their individual initiatives were engaged in planting and stabilising the pillars of British settlements abroad. As John Darwin points out in an illuminating study of the British Empire,

> It was also the case that British expansion had no master-plan. It had almost always been true that colonial schemes or their commercial equivalents were devised not by governments but by private enthusiasts in search of wealth, virtue, or religious redemption. Sometimes they dragged Whitehall in their wake, to get its protection, secure a monopoly or obtain a license to rule through a charter or patent. (3)

A little later Darwin says, "Much more important (than government policies or programs) was the pressure exerted by the old networks and lobbies that managed Britain's overseas interests and the new ones that sprang up to promote commercials, land-seeking, emigrant, humanitarian, missionary or scientific enterprises" (24).

Apart from supplying a corrective to the notion that the British empire was a mighty hegemon, Darwin's words alert us to the wide range of activities that constituted or contributed to imperialism. The commercial factor was of course paramount. The greed of government or private individuals was the main reason why the British clung to overseas possessions with great tenacity for long periods. Someone like Robert Clive may have been working for the East India Company which was also backed by eighteenth-century governments of the day. But he acted quite freely, and amassed huge fortunes as even his

Victorian champion Macaulay acknowledges, writing in 1840: "He lived splendidly, dressed gaily even for those times, kept a carriage and saddle-horses . . ." (500). Later, Macaulay says: ". . . it is also unquestionable that the transactions in which he now began to take part have left a stain on his moral character" (508).

As far as successive British governments were concerned, we have already commented on the way the Industrial Revolution abetted the drive for empire. However, the Industrial Revolution also depended on the success of imperialism for its own perpetuation. The idea was to extract the maximum from the colonies. Talking about the worst of them this is what Conrad has to say: "To tear treasure out of the bowels of the land was their desire, with no more moral purpose at the back of it than there is in burglars breaking into a safe" (177).

Apart from the more brazen forms of oppression such as looting and extorting wealth and valuable merchandise and imposing high taxes on the natives and native products, the Imperial Government also ensured profitability for itself by running the show with as few personnel as possible. While defence-spending was heavy in the Age of the Empire, "in important respects this was an empire on the cheap, superintended by fewer than six thousand administrators as late as the 1880s, profiting from overwhelming military superiority in the face of sporadic indigenous resistance, and policed to a certain extent by an Indian army that was paid for by taxpayers in the sub-continent rather than the metropole (Harling 28). As these lines suggest, the British government and the individual actors who operated with the blessings of the government were simply intent on fleecing the colonies.

This was what empire was all about, although the government did institute certain administrative, social and educational reforms (these also mainly to facilitate governance of large alien territories), and missionaries also gave evidence of genuine philanthropy. There were also those like Edmund Burke in the eighteenth century who stood up for the rights of the oppressed like the Indians when he passionately led the impeachment proceedings against the rapacious viceroy Warren Hastings. In the later part of the nineteenth century the politician Joseph Chamberlain also advocated a humane outlook and liberal politics while dealing with the colonies. However, on the whole the alliance of the military and the merchant class was ruthless and exploitative. The commercial policy was designed to ensure maximum profitability for the British and the military back-up took the form of the army (or the navy with its blockading actions) moving in when commercial interests were threatened.

There were those people like St John Rivers in *Jane Eyre* who waded into the unknown with noble motives. However, his nobility is tinged with racial arrogance and sense of superiority and even a certain selfishness:

> *I* consider that no service degrades which can better our race. I hold that the more arid and unreclaimed the soil [he means a country like India] where the Christian labourer's task of tillage is appointed him – the scantier the meed his toil brings – the higher the honour. His, under such circumstances, is the destiny of the pioneer . . . (428; Ch. 30)

It is that sense of superiority which becomes dangerous when transferred to other spheres of action. Regarding themselves as nobler and better, the British could justify taking lands from the natives and crushing their administrative set-ups. While the missionaries were sometimes critical of the abuses of the colonial administrators, they were sometimes even less sensitive than those abusers. No wonder then that the East India Company was sometimes rather unenthusiastic and even oppositional regarding the zeal displayed by Christian missionaries in spreading their religion in India and trying to do reforms. With the instinct of shrewd conquerors who were here to stay, they realised that there was no point in unnecessarily antagonising the local population.

Imperialism was a diverse practice, encompassing a plethora of activities as enumerated by John Darwin. However, apart from the actual, physical work done (military conquests, building of bridges, railway networks and roads, establishment of Christian missions and schools), another notable factor was that imperialism was a *discourse*, a certain way of seeing, thinking and finally writing or textualising the experience and the mission in the colonies. It was a perpetual story that the colonial planners and executors and all the various champions and apologists of British rule told themselves and told others. Since reports of acts of cruelty and acts violative of British standards of decency and fair play drifted in quite frequently, defenders of empire had to convince themselves and members of the public that it was all right, that nothing was truly amiss. The best spin had to be put on actions that could outrage or baffle; a gloss had to be put on sordid motives. Imperialism as discourse ranged from poems and novels to surveys, reports, travel accounts, diaries, memoirs and letters. Apart from writing about themselves and their motives, the colonisers also had to write about the natives. By acquiring necessary knowledge about the colonised and then giving that knowledge a slant, the colonisers "possessed" the natives and their cultures on the coloniser's own terms. One could say that such writings not only reflected on imperialism, but enacted it. The very circulation of the discourses was part of the ongoing business of empire.

Works of pure imagination that purported to describe imperialism were at one remove from the real business of running the empire. They were often fanciful and also unabashedly propagandist in nature. Some of the less meritorious poems of Victorian poet laureate Alfred Lord Tennyson fall into this category. Patrick Brantlinger quotes Tennyson's poem "Akbar's Dream" (1892) as an instance of imperialist politics. This poem heralds the coming of the great race of the British with all their civilising values:

> but while I groaned,
> from out the sunset poured an alien race,
> who fitted stone to stone again, and Truth, Peace, Love and
> Justice came and dwelt therein,
> Nor in the field without were seen or heard
> Fires of Suttee, nor wails of baby-wife,
> Or Indian widow; ... (Quoted in Brantlinger, *Rule of Darkness* 9)

These words are put in the mouth of Akbar himself, perhaps reflecting the complicity of many Indians in the perpetuation of British rule as well as British pride and conviction about fulfilling their noble destiny in backward oriental lands.

There were other writers who, while not rhetoricising imperial justness or grandness as explicitly as Tennyson, still seemed to be pushing imperial agendas by celebrating the valour of the whites who found themselves in challenging conditions, far away from the ease, comfort and order of home. The depiction of the exploits of the fictional heroes of R. M. Ballantyne and Frederick Marryat as well as the adulation of pre-Victorian Robert Clive and the contemporary David Livingstone are indicators of a craving to revive the notion of heroism in an age of flattening, levelling democracy. (Mario Praz has chronicled the decline of the Victorian hero in a well-known book called *The Hero in Eclipse in Victorian Fiction.*) Carlyle's *Heroes and Hero Worship* (1841), for all its complexity and ingenuity, is a corroboration of this. In the imperial context, heroism entails mastery over other races in inhospitable circumstances. Heroism (incredible that it existed in an age of the aspirations of the dusty, humble proletariat, in an age of painstaking electoral reform carried out to include the participation of all in national life) and colonialism (a very real-enough thing but not something that fired the imagination on a regular basis) could thus be said to complement each other. Talking about the "resurgence of heroes and hero worship," Patrick Brantlinger invokes the example of works such as Charles Kingsley's *Westward Ho*! (1853) and "the burgeoning new industry of boy's adventure tales, started by Captain Marryat (*Rule of Darkness* 36). There is something evasive and simplistic about such heroism, as Brantlinger's words suggest: "Against these complexities (issues of democratic reform and problems of personal and political compromises) which often call for submission to social norms treated as 'laws' of evolution, imperialism offers a swashbuckling politics and a world in which neither epic heroism nor chivalry is dead" (36).

The simplifying tendency evident in the portrayal of heroes intent on planting British flags everywhere is also palpable in the attitudes which were current towards the so-called "inferior" races. Stereotypes, or drastically simplified and falsified images of the natives of conquered lands, were built up in Victorian culture so as to rationalise the occupation of their habitats and the erasure of their ways of life. First of all, there was the myth of blankness or void. It was as if the planet had many empty spaces which were crying out to white conquerors and explorers to come and inhabit and possess. The rivers, mountains, settlements and all other landmarks were deemed nameless, being part of this vast blankness, and had to be given European names so that they come into existence. The iconic Victoria Falls is a persistent reminder of the way the glory of the British crown and empire has been stamped indelibly on the heart of Africa. The idea of certain native populations existing in those blank spaces is admitted, but they are of little real worth. Their religion and culture is as nothing, and they must learn the way of the white invaders or perish. Therefore, even after the "discovery" of indigenous populations, the metaphor of blankness persists at some level of consciousness.

It is this mysterious darkness/emptiness that draws the heroes of H. Rider Haggard, as it drew the real-life heroes such as Stanley, Livingstone, and Cecil Rhodes. Africa was a particularly fascinating and alluring place for the West. The "darkness" acquired a metaphorical density because the people to be explored, invaded, and colonised were themselves dark. The light-skinned whites believed (or made themselves believe) that they carried the torch or beacon of light to these abodes of ignorant and backward races. The black–white opposition became very neat, symmetrical and fulfilling from the Western perspective. In a sense you descended into Hell, but you were an emissary of God and you had the confidence to banish the lurid fire of Hell with heavenly fire, the sacred torch.

The whites simplified the picture to fit the natives and their customs into a pre-determined moral scheme. The people of Asia and Africa (as also the Americas, where, however, it was the Spaniards who were the early conquerors and not the British) were "brutish, false, untrustworthy, and simply the children of a lesser god". Someone like Macaulay was willing to concede that India had an ancient civilisation, but he would also go on to brand Indians as a rather sly and untrustworthy people, without much honour and pride.

The Victorians thought even less of the people of Africa. Even an enlightened feminist such as Harriet Martineau seemed to hold the people of Egypt in great contempt as she travelled through their land. In fact, she seemed to question their very humanity. Discussing her travelogue *Eastern Life* (1848) John Barrell remarks on Martineau's discourse: "a distinction between the modern and the ancient Egyptian seems to do duty also as a distinction between East and West. And it takes the form of denying, sometimes in tones of elaborate disgust, sometimes with a casualness hardly less disturbing, that the Muslim inhabitants of Modern Egypt, . . . are hardly human at all" (188). Martineau's contempt towards non-Western populations is also evident in her *Dawn Island* (1845) where the inhabitants are shown as unenlightened savages.

The revulsion towards Arabs and other Africans is strongly expressed in adventure tales, that genre which thrived on East–West encounters in the nineteenth century. This is how the British servant Job in H. Rider Haggard's novel *She* (1886) feels about the Moslems who accompany him with his masters in their expedition into Africa: "I don't think it would matter if it did (that the moon might turn his head or blind him), it is that turned already with the sight of these blackamoors and their filthy, thieving ways. They are only fit for muck, they are; and they smell bad enough for it already" (47; Ch. 4).

As Job is depicted as a good, loyal character in the novel, his views cannot but reflect his author's to some extent. Thus these instances from a travelogue by a serious reformist and a novel by a popular adventure writer show the depth and intensity of racism that existed among the British, and that came to the surface when they dealt with the subject of empire in some way.

It fell to the late Victorian writer Rudyard Kipling to coin the most telling phrase in this drama of the assertion of white superiority to justify the gigantic enterprise of imperialism/colonialism. He wrote his famous poem, "The White Man's Burden" (1899), to lend his support to American imperialism in general, and specifically, perhaps to the American effort to annex the Philippines around the turn of the century, and the title of the poem has been resonating in discussions of colonial politics and colonial hegemony There are interesting, unsuspected affinities between Kipling and Conrad – another commentator on late imperialism. As Conrad does the robust and disciplined cannibals in *Heart of Darkness,* Kipling seems to admire certain strong, honourable men of the East in several of his works. Both are complex writers with a deep knowledge about human nature on the "other" side. Kipling might be an apologist or a champion of Western imperialism, but he was not blind to the folly, greed and arrogance of the white man as can be seen in a novella such as *The Man Who Would be King* (1888). Daniel Dravot, the protagonist of this work, is actually someone who tries to be both god and king. The title fits an overreacher such as Kurtz of *Heart of Darkness.* On the other hand, the "idea" that Conrad (through Marlow) sees as the only justification for white presence in a land where whites have otherwise no business to be, sounds a lot like Kipling's infamous white man's burden. While we will have a little more to say about Conrad to do justice to his pioneering anti-colonialism, about Kipling it would be safe to say that like some other lesser writers of his age, he subscribed to the theory of Western superiority which placed almost a divine obligation and a moral 'burden' on the whites to rule the brown, black and yellow people of the earth.

There were also those in the Victorian era and in the nineteenth century generally who, without being consciously racist, espoused theories which made connection between notions of racial superiority and the right to colonial or imperial domination. None other than Charles Darwin himself laid down the theory about certain races inevitably perishing because they were unfit to survive. He did this in a detached, objective way, and his theory of extinction in no way reflected any belief about might being right or the greater right of some races to rule. During his actual travels he was pained by the frequent sight of colonial brutality in various places of South America. Nevertheless, Darwin's progressive scientific ideas became Social Darwinism, a belief system that was not really faithful to Darwin's humane postulations about the nature of existence on this planet. Patrick Brantlinger's *Dark Vanishings* continues with the exposés of imperial iniquities that one sees in *Rule of Darkness,* but in the later work he interrogates scientific racism which actually began in the eighteenth century and continued throughout the nineteenth and beyond. This brand of racism also has as its basic premise the survival of the fittest which was at the heart of Darwin's work as also of the works of his predecessors and contemporaries. However, while Darwin and others like him were mainly concerned with actions in the plant and animal world, the proponents of scientific racism dealt with the interaction of human races.

Many Victorian authors either aired racist views in letters or prose works or built narratives on foundations of imperial justification or white supremacy. Patrick Brantlinger calls these "extinction discourses." He gives the example of a pre-Darwinian scientist named Georges Curvier in this context. Curvier points to what he sees as the beautiful form of the head Caucasian variety from which "have sprung the most civilized nations." In contrast the "negro race" with its "compressed cranium" resembles the monkey tribe and has always been in a state of barbarism (Brantlinger, *Dark Vanishings* 20). There were many others who held similar views. The parliamentary radical J. A. Roebuck has this to say about the inevitable demise of certain races in a work entitled *The Colonies of England* (1849): "I say, that for the mass, the sum of human enjoyment to be derived from this globe which God has given to us, it is requisite for us to pass over the original tribes that we find existing in the separate lands which we colonize . . . . When the European comes in contact with any other type of man, that other type disappears . . . ." (qtd in Brantlinger, *Dark Vanishings* 6).

There are a few other interesting dimensions to the subject of imperialism and racism that may be briefly considered. Many critics have pointed out that it was not a wholesale superiority of one race over another that constituted the totality of the imperial consciousness or unconscious. There is the class issue, for instance, which complicates matters. Many who went and obtained coveted posts in the colonial administration (and thus truly felt themselves to be a master race) were from upper-class families and had obtained advantageous education from renowned public schools. But there were many whites who landed up in the colonies and settled there but did not enjoy such privileged backgrounds. It is doubtful whether all of them felt racially superior to the black, brown or yellow natives all the time. As Ann Laura Stoler points out,

> Some European colonial men would have numbered themselves within that class (a superior body with power and rights) but not others. Some may have characterised themselves as having "power and influence" over the native population, but not over other Europeans. Still others . . . were only too well aware of their dubious command over "the natives", and their limited mastery over themselves. (91–92)

It seemed that the same arrogance that created mental barriers between the ruling classes in England and the lower/working classes in England was at work in delineating the relationship between the coloniser and the colonised. Apart from certain cherished slots in the colonial bureaucracy or army, the colonies were not necessarily very congenial places to be. The perspective about "blank spaces" meant that many of these were treated as trash-spilling sites. As with the progression of medical science birth rates grew and death rates fell in Victorian England without a corresponding spike in employment opportunities, forced migrations seemed to be a good solution to rid the nation of unwanted, potentially turbulent and rebellious elements. There is a hint of "racism" in the anti-poor, tyrannous Lord Marney's assertion in *Sybil*: "Nothing can put this country right but emigration on a great scale; and as the government does not choose to undertake it, I have commenced it for my own defence on a small scale. I will take care that the population of my parishes is not increased" (109; Bk 2, Ch. 2). This sounds somewhat like today's ethnic cleansing, except that Marney is referring to his own race. There was a more literal racism in the global narrative of immigration and emigration in Britain. Many emigrants *to* Britain were the poor Irish, who came in desperate search of employment and livelihood. Many Englishmen, including well-known authors such as Charles Kingsley, harboured attitudes of extreme disdain and revulsion towards them, regarding them as animal-like, despite being white. It would not be incorrect to say that such attitudes to working-class populaces were exported to the colonies to keep the indigenous people under foot. There is thus cogency in Patrick Brantlinger's view that "racism functions as a displaced or surrogate class system . . . imperialist discourse treats class and race terminology as covertly interchangeable or at least analogous" (*Rule of Darkness* 184). Historian Victor Kiernan also makes the analogical connection, pointing to contemporary attitudes of class and race prejudice in the book *The Lords of Human Kind*: "Discontented native in the colonies, labour agitator in the mills, were the same serpent in alternate disguise" (qtd in Stoler 105).

There is another aspect of imperial sociology and politics that needs to be pointed out if we are to make out the case that imperial or colonial identity was not such a stable or secure business, with all whites on the "right" side of the power and prestige divide. The nabobs may have enjoyed privileges and gathered wealth in places like the Indian empire, but were often misfits back home. William Thackeray who was born in India and had an acute class consciousness regarding these matters creates a nabob figure in the person of the repelling Jos Sedley. Satirically called the collector of Bogleywallah, Sedley is pursued by the scheming Becky Sharp and he finally falls prey to her almost literally, as there is a strong suggestion that he is killed by her at the end. The pathetic, insecure, cowardly Jos is a far cry from the likes of earlier and real-life nabobs such as Clive with their swagger and superior sense, although the fact remains that all nabobs had problems of adjustment in home society after stints in the empire where they commanded homage and instant obedience. Making Jos fat and cowardly is Thackeray's way of saying, along with many others, that the hero had vanished from the landscape even though the British continued to be the conquering race. (The sub-title of *Vanity Fair* is "A Novel Without a Hero".)

The colonists were not always above and occupying a clearly demarcated mental space away from the natives whom they ruled. This is a point most famously made by Edward Said when he talks about the Orient as Europe's "Other." Many other modern critics, including the ones I have used here have talked about white fears about a secret affinity with all those filthy colonised legions. It goes with the Victorian flirtation with the notion of a secret or buried self, first made famous by Mathew Arnold in a poem called "The Buried Life." Sometimes there are feelings that this unofficial self, this hidden part of the identity is the *real* self which emerges under pressure or during moments of crisis. John Barrell invokes recent critical works in this area as support for his own argument about it: "There has been an attempt . . . to focus more closely on the operations of fantasy and projection, and to talk about that attitude of disgust towards the Other which is always a self-disgust, about the Western fear of the Oriental, including the Jew, as a fear of something inside the Western psyche, something which is imperfectly repressed or is even produced by the civilizing process" (188–89).

Thus the British feared that the colonist would "go native" and degenerate, becoming like those wretched creatures with whom they were forced to mingle while being some part of the empire-building project. Under extreme pressure their lower self, which might truthfully be the *real* self, might break through and emerge. *Heart of Darkness* (1899) is a modern work par excellence in many ways, but its chronology makes it a commentary on Victorian practices from within Victorian times. No other British text has better captured the very real degeneration of the Europeans as they went about plundering a continent while hiding behind the noble rhetoric of philanthropy.

Apart from touching on the issues of the secret self and the kinship between "civilised" whites and "uncivilised" Africans, the work explodes many cherished Victorian myths regarding progress, enlightenment and manliness. Applying incipient modernist techniques such as fragmentary discourse and open-endedness, Conrad in *Heart of Darkness* also anticipates postmodern or poststructuralist trends such as the subversion of enduring cultural binaries and the problematic nature of seeking for knowledge which often ends up with the realisation of the futility of such knowledge-quests. However, in content this is very much an Age of Empire book. More than any other nineteenth century work *Heart* deals directly with the issues of empire and its bitter, harrowing aftermath. But if it is argued that the central character of Kurtz in this novella is too complex a case to be made representative of the degenerating European in the sweeping amphitheatre of the empire, the examples of the sickly Kayerts and Carlier in *An Outpost of Progress* (1897) can be more readily and convincingly invoked. These two characters, colonial functionaries seemingly representing Belgium but standing for all of degenerate colonialism, simply disintegrate at the end and go for each other's lives.

Because of the lack of the visibility of empire, and also because of the predominance of domestic issues such as love, courtship, marriage and property settlements (in certain works religion and industrial unrest jostled these domestic subjects for space), it may seem that the empire was not an everyday issue for the public. It was not also a popular topic for writers either except the odd occasion when "official" poets such as Tennyson saw it fit to trumpet British imperial might and rightness in poems such as "Akbar's Dream."

Indeed, writing in the heyday of the Victorian period, Macaulay found himself lamenting the lack of interest in imperial issues:

> It might have been expected, that every Englishman who takes any interest in any part of history would be curious to know how a handful of his countrymen, separated from their home by an immense ocean, subjugated in the course of a few years, one of the greatest empires in the world. Yet, unless we greatly err, this subject is, to most readers, not only insipid, but positively distasteful. (479)

As the empire and its history were always uppermost in Lord Macaulay's mind, it not being the most popular of subjects in public discourses would naturally disappoint him. But the business of empire actually underwrote everything, and traces of it may be found in writings which may apparently be about all other kinds of things. By colonising large parts of the world and dominating international trade and commerce, Victorian England was often the hub, transit point, or centre for ceaseless arrivals and departures, inflows and outflows of people engaged with different colonial ventures. Many of the novels of the period glance at colonial mobility and traffic. Sometimes the (escape to) empire even becomes a solution to narrative entanglements. In many such dealings with the empire, writers neither condemn nor celebrate imperialism. It is a fact of life, like many others.

In *David Copperfield* the perennially struggling Micawber seems to be rewarded for being an essentially good person by being bestowed a governorship in Australia. Australia was a settler nation, swiftly populated by large droves of emigrants from the British Isles. Sometimes the exoduses from the mother country were planned affairs. As Darwin points out, "The South Australian Association was a highly successful lobby that won government support for a new settlement colony to which more than 10,000 migrants were sent in its first few years"(43). Large droves also made their way to Canada and New Zealand in similar fashion. Apart from fulfilling individual aspirations, the idea behind such ventures was to spread ideals of Britishness in different parts of the world.

Sometimes such exiles and exoduses had a darker tinge. From at least the eighteenth century many convicts were transported to the settler nations, the Americas or other colonies, and prevented from returning on pain of death. Moll Flanders, in the novel of the same name by Defoe (1722), is famously transported to America for her misdeeds. Hetty Sorrel in Eliot's *Adam Bede* escapes being hanged for killing her illegitimate baby but is transported instead. (It is a different matter that for the moral Eliot Hetty's real punishment is the last cry of the baby that haunts Hetty.) In Dickens's *Great Expectations* Magwitch (like Micawber, a father or uncle figure to the protagonist) also finds himself in Australia. But unlike Micawber, his exile is ignominious, as he is transported as a convicted felon. Interestingly, both Micawber and Magwitch prosper, the first as an administrator and the latter as sheep-raiser and stock-breeder. However, Magwitch chooses to return from exile and the consequences of this return point to the complexities of Britain's imperial connections. With the money that Magwitch earns, he sponsors Pip's career of becoming a gentleman. While the gesture itself is noble, and an indication of how the finest human impulses may survive in unfavourable circumstances, the money is tainted because it is illegally sent by a convicted offender. Pip realises this to his horror and dismay, and the project of being a gentleman collapses. Inevitably this puts a question mark on the wealth that poured in from abroad and brought prosperity to people's lives.

Wealth with imperial associations is also at least a subsidiary concern in Trollope's *The Eustace Diamonds* (1871). Here also, issues of affluence, ambition and morality are involved, although in a somewhat different way from how these issues are portrayed in the novels of Dickens. At the heart of the plot is the alleged stealing of diamonds by the villainess/protagonist Lizzie. The parodically named Indian prince Sawab of Mygawb is robbed, providing the work with its "imperial" connection. In fact, the editor of the text W. J. McCormack calls Anthony Trollope "*the* imperial novelist" in his introduction to *The Eustace Diamonds* (xii). He draws our attention to Trollope's long stint in Ireland as a colonial official as well as his travels in settler nations such as Australia to back up his claim. But more importantly for his argument, Trollope connects characters and their petty concerns with the global world. This is in line with the point we are making about the non-explicit or unobtrusive nature of imperial themes in Victorian literature. As Lizzie steals from the Sawab, to her "are drawn all those evidences of the world beyond England" (xxx). McCormack also makes this comment: "India has been the subject of many of 'Mr Burke's speeches,' and the robbery of India at that too" (xxiv).

Thackeray's *Vanity Fair* (1848) also has many evidences "of the world beyond England." In many ways it is a more obviously imperial novel than Trollope's work. A work with a sweeping canvas, it deals with the Napoleonic War, and has minor characters from profitable colonies from the West Indies and India in the persons of the heiress Miss Swartz and the pathetic servant of Jos Sedley called the Bengalee. The race association with imperialism that we have been noticing also comes in with these characters. Thackeray is throughout playfully ironic and critical regarding individuals and their motives as well as the decadence of British institutions and classes. However, the playfulness over Miss Swartz's skin colour, although not attributable to the implied author's perspective, still disturbs us. It is almost as if unlike Conrad, Thackeray is anti-imperialist but not anti-racist, if that is possible.

Miss Swartz's brief presence in the novel helps to connect domestic subjects such as courtship and marriage to the exotic world of the colonies which represented great wealth and nothing more for the British. Her lack of physical attractiveness (due to skin colour) is made apparent. This highlights the fact that she is just a prize or commodity to be won, with no intrinsic value or life of her own. It is almost as if she is a symbol of the exploited colony.

And then there is Jos Sedley, about whom we have already spoken, and whom Robert Polhemus aptly brands "a fleshbag of conspicuous consumption" who "mirrors the grotesque side of British imperialism" (141). If Swartz is a symbol of the exploited colony, Sedley can be seen as a symbol of the exploiting colonial power which fattens itself at the expense of the colonies. It may well be that through this fat, cowardly Englishman, the collector of Boggleywallah, Thackeray was making an indictment of British imperialism. Trollope only travelled through the colonies, but Thackeray was born in one: India. The main critical thrust of this novel is directed at the avarice and luxury-loving ways of the British upper classes. As in Trollope's works, and as also in real life, the upper classes were losing their vitality largely because they indulged themselves with unearned income wrested from colonies such as India.

While some criticism of greed-based British imperialism underlines quite a few of the above works, it can be argued that Wilkie Collins's detective-adventure novel, *The Moonstone,* is the strongest, and clearest indictment of "imperial thievery." While in Victorian times there was a denial or suppression of the connection between home life and the business of empire, modern critics have unveiled that connection. They have also demonstrated that the connection does not reflect any credit on how the British perceived their roles vis-à-vis the colonies. There is now fresh evaluation of Victorian texts in the light of the recognition that the business of empire was more unsavoury and greedy, and far less heroic, philanthropic and progressive than what its apologists would have people believe.

Collins's *The Moonstone* (1868) is set in England, and highlights various domestic matters such as inheritances, family relationships and courtship and marriage, much like many other contemporary novels. It is also a sensation novel dealing with robbery and killing, mysterious strangers, intruders, detectives, and family secrets of the kind greatly popular in the Victorian age. (The writings of Willkie Collins themselves contributed to the popularity of this genre.) However, this is a colonial novel as much as it is a crime novel. Through this novel, Willkie Collins mounts an assault on British attitudes and policies towards its colonies. Melissa Free's comments help us in seeing the centrality of empire in the life of the nation: "To 'be' English in the nineteenth century was to be of, and hence constituted by (the British) empire, to claim the summary position not only of Britishness but of empire itself" (340).

It was not just the government and its colonial servants which reached out to the colonies and dealt with them. In some ways, all the citizens were participants in the colonial project. Even if ordinary English men and women were not concerned with the empire on a daily basis, the government could not colonise and administer without the connivance or backing of the public at home. Also, everyone benefited from the exploitation of the wealth and resources of the colonies, and so everyone was morally compromised if not actually contaminated.

The imperial imagination often depicts Indians and other "Asiatics" and "Orientals" as thieving and untrustworthy. A case in point is the attitude harboured by the man Job towards his fellow Muslim expeditionists in the novel *She*. These men are also regarded as heathens and thus associated with the devil whom in some form they worship. In *The Moonstone* three mysterious Indians prowl around in the city and in the countryside, and when a valuable diamond is stolen from the home of the wealthy Lady Verinder, they are suspects. Finally they do steal the diamond and take it back to India. The diamond itself, the moonstone of the title, is called "devilish" by the narrator/ character Betteredge: "Here was our quiet English house suddenly invaded by a devilish Indian diamond – bringing after it a conspiracy of living rogues, set loose on us by the vengeance of a dead man" (Collins, Ch.5). The perspectives of this and other characters reinforce stereotypes about India. The diamond is a curse from India, afflicting hapless English men and women. As critics such as Free have shown, the diamond is *plundered* rather than cursed. Before the Indians try to steal it back, the diamond was stolen by an Englishman named John Herncastle in 1799 in the siege of Seringapatam. The Indians are Brahmins who are hereditary custodians of the sacred moonstone which nestles in the forehead of the moon god in Somnath before it was stolen by Mahmud of Ghazni. Now these custodians are only trying to reclaim what belongs to India. The novel is rare in its near-total sympathy for the Indian cause and perspective. Collins's narrative can be seen as emblematic of the entire imperial venture, which was a scandal and an extended act of thievery or brigandage. As Mellisa Free says, "In my analysis, empire, not the Moonstone, is the family curse and the real 'family scandal', centred around – and illuminated by – the spoils of empire, is the scandal of a grasping nation overreaching itself, protected by the urgency of containment from within. Family history operates as imperial history writ small . . ." (348).

The typical Victorian narrative gesture was to relate everything to everything else, and their plots rested on visible and invisible affinities and causal relations. This practice is most apparent in long multi-plot novels with their crisscrossing plot lines, but in this compact novel too this narrative principle seems to be operational. Collins relates seemingly quiet domesticity to turmoil abroad, and shows how the blood-letting and unrest prevalent in foreign lands is actually caused by the attitudes of English men and women far removed from the scenes of strife. The entire story of empire is one that the British liked to hear from a safe distance, and like the family of Lady Verinder in *The Moonstone,* they ignore, evade and suppress all knowledge and insight that is unpalatable or inconvenient. The empire is a tissue of lies, and it squats on an edifice of injustice: "the murders and the thefts that the family tries to keep quiet serve as a cloak for a murderous, thieving nation, generating and purportedly preserving its empire" (343).

Many instances can be found whereby the empire creeps into or flickers in many Victorian narratives without occupying centre-stage. Faced with insoluble problems of survival, many people, like the main characters Mary and Jem at the end of Gaskell's *Mary Barton* (1848), emigrate to the different parts of the empire. At the end of Gaskell's *Sylvia's Lovers* too, a character is shown as having emigrated to America. Alton Locke in the novel of that name emigrates to America but dies right after reaching his destination. These are instances where the empire with its varied scenes comes in handy as narrative resolution, which reflected actual happenings. Apart from long and permanent emigrations such as the ones mentioned here, there were trips made by characters who come back after enriching themselves. The great canvas of the empire was profitable, not just to governments, government functionaries, agents of empire and various merchants and soldiers of fortune, but to writers as well. We see how writers profitably and productively use imperial themes even when their concerns are not directly with empire-building and empire-running.

Works Cited

Barrell, John. "Death on the Nile: Fantasy and the Literature of Tourism, 1840–60." Ed. Catherine Hall. *Cultures of Empire: Colonizers in Britain and the Empire in the Nineteenth and Twentieth Centuries: A Reader*. Manchester: Manchester UP, 2000. 187–203. Print.

Brantlinger, Patrick. *Rule of Darkness: British Literature and Imperialism, 1830–1914*. Ithaca and London: Cornell UP, 1990. Print.

———. *Dark Vanishings: Discourse on the Extinction of Primitive Races, 1800–1930*. Ithaca and London: Cornell UP, 2003. Print.

Brontë, Charlotte. *Jane Eyre.* Ware, Hertfordshire: Wordsworth Classics Limited, 1992. Print.

Collins, Wilkie. *The Moonstone.* Project Gutenberg. Web. 22 June 2016. <http://www.gutenberg.org/ebooks>.

Conrad, Joseph. *Heart of Darkness and Other Tales.* Oxford: Oxford UP, 1992. Print. Oxford World's Classics.

Darwin, John. *The Empire Project: The Rise and Fall of the British World-System 1830–1970.* Cambridge: Cambridge UP, 2009. Print.

Disraeli, Benjamin. *Sybil OR The Two Nations.* Oxford: Oxford UP, 2008. Print. Oxford World's Classics.

Free, Melissa. " 'Dirty Linen': Legacies of Empire in Wilkie Collins's *The Moonstone.*" *Texas Studies in Literature and Language* 48. 4 (Winter 2006): 340–71. Project Muse. Web. 28 May 2015. <http://muse.jhu.edu/article/209032>.

Hall, Catherine. *Cultures of Empire: Colonizers in Britain and the Empire in the Nineteenth and Twentieth Centuries: A Reader.* Manchester: Manchester UP, 2000. Print.

Harling, Philip. "The Powers of the Victorian State." *Liberty and Authority in Victorian Britain.* Ed. Peter Mandler. Oxford: Oxford UP, 2006. 25–51. Print.

Hobsbawm, Eric. *The Age of Empire: 1875–1914.* New York: Vintage Books, 1989. Print.

Macaulay, Thomas Babington. "Lord Clive."*Critical and Historical Essays.* Volume One. London: J. M. Dent, 1963. 479–549. Print. Everyman's Library.

McCormack, W. J. "Introduction." *The Eustace Diamonds.* Oxford: Oxford UP, 1983. xi–xxxii. Print. The World's Classics.

Polhemus, Robert. *Comic Faith: The Great Tradition from Austen to Joyce.* Chicago: U of Chicago P, 1980. Print.

Rider Haggard, H. *She.* London: Hodder and Stoughton, 1951. Print.

Stein, Burton. *A History of India*. New Delhi: Oxford UP, 2006. Print.

Stoler, Ann Laura. "Cultivating Bourgeois Bodies and Racial Selves." Hall. 87–119.

Tennyson, Alfred. "Akbar's Dream." Patrick Brantlinger. 9. Print.

Webb, Igor. *From Custom to Capital: The English Novel and the Industrial Revolution*. Ithaca and London: Cornell UP, 1981. Print.

FIVE

The Woman Question

Many sensitive and frustrated women of the Victorian period wondered, like Caroline Helstone in the novel *Shirley*, as to what they could *do* in life to have a sense of meaning and fulfilment in society. Writers such as Caroline's creator Charlotte Brontë and George Eliot yearned to face situations which would challenge their abilities. However, they (and their protagonists) were unable to do so because of the numerous restrictive codes, conventions and customs in Victorian society that laid down hurdles in their paths.

What could a woman really do? Where could she found fulfilment? The question that Robert Moore poses to the woman who loves him, is applicable across the board, to women of various backgrounds and classes: "What life are you destined for, Caroline?" (70; Ch. 5). Caroline's brave reply, that she would like to be apprenticed to a cloth trade, reflects early signs of feminist stirrings but seems to be lacking in the spirit of practical reality. Strange, haunting contradictions about women's lot confront an observer even when he surveys the social scene late in the century. The New Woman had arrived then and they demanded an honourable place under the sun for all women. But to borrow the title of George Gissing's oddly disturbing book *The Odd Women* (1893), apart from the confident feministic New Women there were many others too whom society found difficult to fit into the scheme of things. This was the woman who was the "odd man" out, the one who was a surplus or excess (half a million more than the men, as one of the characters in the book says) – outside the working social economy. For them life is bleak and unrelieved by flashes of glorious possibilities of womanhood that elevate someone like Dorothea in *Middlemarch* even when the latter feels tied down by the pressures of provincial life. In the words of Helen Rogers, "Without the means of self-culture and independence in the home or as citizens, they were reduced to a state of *de facto* enslavement" (132).

It is not as if the condition of women sharply deteriorated over the course of the century. To the contrary, it improved in many respects. As for the "oddness," even earlier in the period, the condition of women was always afflicted by an imbalance. Those who could, found a husband for themselves and things "evened" out for them. The ones left stranded in the outer darkness – various restricted zones and social margins – were the odd women, unmatched to any supporting male. There was no dearth of such superfluous women in the Victorian period. The 1851 census revealed to a shocked nation that there many more unmarried women than they had thought, a fact that seemed a blow to the family idyll central to Victorian culture.

The women who did not find any husbands for themselves were doubly damned. As in the case of the Madden sisters in *The Odd Women,* life was a dreary business, a time of long privations when the first provider, the father, died early and the next one, the husband did not appear on the horizon. Then the husbandless women bore the social stigma of being unnatural creatures. This was because the Victorian domestic ideology thrived on the iteration of the "angelic" role played by woman as daughter, wife, and mother. This role of the domestic angel was the one true vocation, universally endorsed. All other possibilities were out of reach or were frowned upon in a country which was, ironically enough, ruled by a woman. The absolute antithesis of the angel, the demon/witch also bothered or haunted the Victorian imagination. That is to say, not everyone was convinced that angelhood was innate in woman. And this made the celebration of the angel of the domestic variety even more urgent. Guidebooks and conduct manuals hemmed women in from all sides and curtailed the scope of their activities even when they pursued their innocuous, inoffensive activities sanctioned by society. About the angel figure, however, a little more will be said later in this essay.

Apart from being the presiding deity in the domestic sphere (specifically, within familial confines), what other options were open to women? There were no "she-bishops" except in the satirical sense in which Trollope employed the term, indicating a bossy, interfering woman such as Mrs Proudie in *Barchester Towers* who rules from the shadows. They could hardly be explorers, university professors, soldiers, civil servants or colonial administrators. Somehow, despite the external disapprovals and the inner inhibitions, some women managed to sneak through the barricades to adopt "manly" pursuits such as science. There *were* actually women scientists, doctors and engineers, whose achievements were however, not widely recognised. In any case, there would not be so many of them in early and mid-Victorian periods that being a scientist was a viable career. If women felt the fascination of scientific views then sweeping the nation, the most they could was read science and like George Eliot, write scientific narratives. Mental barriers made the pursuit or adoption of challenging and strenuous career options rather difficult.

She could be a nurse, but rarely a doctor. However, while the aura surrounding a nurse was soothing and ennobling, the reality was often sordid and degrading. Again, we can go to the mordant wit and wisdom of Strachey for the restoration of perspectives. "But the particular profession for which Florence was clearly marked out both by her instincts and her capacities was at that time a peculiarly disreputable one. A 'nurse' meant then a coarse old woman, always ignorant, usually dirty, often brutal, a Mrs Gamp (a comic but disreputable character in Dickens's novel), in bunched-up sordid garments, tippling at the brandy bottle or indulging in worse irregularities" (85). Interestingly, in Strachey's hands Florence Nightingale's achievement was that she became an intermediate figure: neither the angelic icon of the myth-making imagination, nor the coarse and unappetising figure identified by Strachey.

Apart from these, there were the occupations of seamstresses and weavers – the kind of occupation that was synonymous with never-ending toil and scant reward in a gray world of pain, privations and almost physical obscurity. Ruth and her friends, the dressmakers' apprentices, endlessly harassed by the slave-driving Mrs Mason in Elizabeth Gaskell's novel, *Ruth* (1853), "stitching away as if for very life, not daring to gape, or show any outward manifestation of sleepiness" (2; Ch. 1) are examples of this category of unfortunates. There was also the household help, like that of the Marchioness treated harshly by a particularly malignant mistress in *The Old Curiosity Shop.* Slightly higher up the ladder, there were the possibilities of teachers and governesses.

These two "careers" seemed tailor-made for genteel, intelligent women. Both seemed to be suitable (sometimes a governess was also a teacher – for just the children of the family with whom she would be staying) and in keeping with the peculiar abilities of women. In reality the situation was less than ideal. The figure of the governess particularly troubled the Victorian imagination. Going by bare statistics, the governess could not be regarded as a particularly significant figure. After all, there were not all that many governesses at any point of time, and as M. Jeanne Peterson points out, they were much less in numbers than female domestic servants and women employed in industries (4). Nevertheless, the plight of the governess engaged people's sympathetic attention because of the feeling that circumstances had dragged many women of genteel families down from their social stations and forced them to drudge in a way that did not do justice to their talents or their birth. The governess question (as also many other career options) was in a way linked to the turmoil of a progressing but unstable time-period. Fluctuations of fortune might compel a woman to climb down a few steps and toil in someone else's house. There were, however, also governesses who were from the lower classes although one does not read about too many of them in the fiction of the period.

Certainly a thesis about refined women coming down in the world seems relevant in the lives of the Brontës. Daughters of a respectable parson, with expectations of being well-mannered young ladies, they were confronted with hardship especially when their father's health declined. In fact, many of the revelations made in *The Life of Charlotte Brontë* show how the Brontë sisters in their real lives had to confront choices and challenges that were more trying and drearier (at least when it came to livelihood matters) than what greeted Catherine Earnshaw in *Wuthering Heights*, and Shirley Keeldar in *Shirley*, two of the more affluent female protagonists in the Brontë fictional world.

The Life of Charlotte Brontë by Elizabeth Gaskell is quite remarkable for the way it lays out the paucity of career choices for women of genteel but hard-up families. Gaskell fills her work with many evidential writings such as letters by Charlotte to various people. This is how Charlotte describes the contents of a letter from Emily who had gone to teach in a school at Halifax: ". . . it gives an appalling account of her duties; hard labour from six in the morning to eleven at night, with only one half-hour of exercise between. This is slavery. I fear she can never stand it" (96; Ch. 8). The Brontës try their hands at being governesses too. However, being a governess brings in scant rewards in a regime of great demands and expectations on the part of the employers: the parents of the often unmanageable children whom the governesses were meant to tutor and generally look after. About the ordeal of being a governess, this is what Charlotte has to say: "But no one but myself can tell how hard a governess's work is to me – for no one but myself is aware how utterly averse my whole mind and nature are for the employment" (135; 8). She also gives the reasons for the aversion: "If teaching only were requisite, it would be smooth and easy; but it is the living in other people's houses – the estrangement from one's real character – the adoption of a cold, rigid, apathetic exterior, that is painful" (139–40).

While the most famous governesses in Victorian literature are to be found in works written by the Brontës, works such as *Agnes Grey* (1847), and *Jane Eyre*, the governess makes an appearance in the works of other writers too, including male writers. Sometimes a male author is seen to extract whole-hearted sympathy and compassion for a governess. Such a one is Lucy Morris in Trollope's *The Eustace Diamonds*. Unlike many other real or fictional governesses, Lucy is able to climb out of the depressed class of the governess, essentially being rewarded for her goodness by the author. In general, however, male writers are not able to evince the same kind of sympathetic feeling for (or sense of identification with) a governess as a woman writer. Also, the governesses in such cases are marginal to the main narrative or a female protagonist is seen to take up the profession only briefly. Someone like Mrs General makes only a brief appearance in *Little Dorrit*, and she imparts futile and even damaging education to the Dorrit children. Becky Sharp in *Vanity Fair* is briefly a governess, and in that brief stint she inculcates subversive ideas in her ward, the children of the Crawley establishment. She is certainly no advertisement for the perfect and happy vocation of the governess.

The vocation of being a *writer* was ideal, but could hardly be regarded as a widely-available, viable career choice. It is true, however, that a woman could actually earn money by selling her works to publishers and to editors of literary journals and magazines. Also, through the medium of writing, a woman could reach out and connect with many people, something which was otherwise not possible, given the various social limitations of a Victorian woman in matters of mobility and movements in the public realm. However, a woman writer had to advance in her chosen path in the face of disheartening opposition put up by some male writers. One of the more famous instances of this is the exhortation by the poet laureate Robert Southey to Charlotte Bronte to do her woman's duties rather than aspire to be a writer when the latter asks him for advice and encouragement. This episode is also recorded by Mrs Gaskell in her biography of Brontë.

While Victorian works of literature would often illuminate whatever variety of roles women were allowed to play out, in a very fundamental sense, all their works, however, had to do with the position of women within the family and with domestic ideology in general. Guidebook writers such as Sarah Ellis had a big role for women (middle-class women in particular), a regulatory, supervisory role within familial parameters. Ellis says that educated women should be honoured to increase happiness because they spread their educated manners through the household and goes on to say that "it is to the indefatigable exertion and faithful labours of women of this class, that England chiefly owes the support of some of her noblest and most benevolent institutions" (27; Ch. 1).

The family was, of course, of central importance for the Victorians. Not only was it seen as a place where crucial norms and values could be nurtured, it was also an emotional sanctuary providing a moral counter to negative developments elsewhere. As Leonore Davidoff and Catherine Hall point out,

> Writing in the troubled decades of the 1830s and 1840s, when political and social unrest both at home and abroad was rife, they (the conservative Ellis and the more radical Harriet Martineau)

> propagandized for the family as a repository of stability and firm values . . . At a time when some socialists and feminists were seeking new forms of marriage and new kinds of relations between men and women, these thinkers were arguing for a stable family as the way to achieve not only social harmony but also individual fulfilment. (309)

Religious schism and other disintegrating tendencies made the need for buttressing the moral structure of the home acuter as it could symbolically represent a well-ordered government, free of dissent and strife. In fact, while the portals to many social, political, and religious institutions were closed to women, they were supposedly supreme within the confines of the family. However, this supremacy could be illusory; the granting of pride of place to women in the domestic sphere could be seen as a subtle strategy to keep them away from more meaningful participation in a rapidly evolving world which was seeing the opening up of different careers and vocational opportunities all the time. As the Industrial Revolution made its impact felt more and more, the sense of the family as a sanctuary or a shrine grew. With the boundary between public and private, home and elsewhere becoming sharper, it was deemed proper for women to be the presiding deities at home. Their domestic virtues and apparent powers were extolled even more, thus freezing women in their "homely" stations. This was more so in the case of middle and upper-class women. Working-class women had to venture outside to supplement meagre family incomes; there was little choice here. Late in the century, however, the image of the family declined due to many factors and this is also reflected in works of the period which present greater realism in the portrayals of women.

In the mid-Victorian period, it was Coventry Patmore who was responsible for exalting woman in her domestic role and thus contributing to a certain kind of woman-centred domesticity. His poem, *Angel in the House* (1854–56), was famous at that time and still continues to enjoy a dubious fame today as critics interrogate different versions of the angel in the house scattered through the writings of diverse Victorian writers. Lines such as the following set a burdensome template for the portrayal of angelic domesticity although such an ideology of domestic spirituality (or spiritual domesticity) had already existed:

> Her disposition is devout,
> Her countenance angelical;
> The best things that the best believe
> Are in her face so kindly writ
> The faithless, seeing her, conceive
> Not only heaven, but hope of it
> . . . (Canto IV ll.11–17)

To take but just one earlier example for the time being, in *David Copperfield*, there is a chapter entitled "Good and Bad Angels." The good angel here is Agnes, whom David associates with all that is holy and pure: "I cannot call to mind where or when, in my childhood, I had seen a stained glass window in a church . . . But I know that when I saw her turn around, in the grave light of the old staircase, and wait for us, above, I thought of that window; and I associated something of its tranquil brightness with Agnes Wickfield ever afterwards" (280; Bk 5; Ch. 15) . Apart from transporting David to a purer world, Agnes has to bear the symbolic burden of being the good angel in a world peopled by "bad angels" such as Uriah Heep.

John Ruskin, an outstanding voice against injustice in the Victorian age, was one of those responsible for the hardening of the angel in the house myth. With Ruskin, as with other Victorian thinkers, the interesting thing was that he saw women as he wanted to see them rather than as women were – with all their problems and possibilities. In the essay "The Debate Over Women: Ruskin vs. Mill," Kate Millet argues that John Stuart Mill's rationalistic defence of women's rights was more beneficial to women's emancipation than the irrational, romantic elevation of women by Ruskin. Reacting to what he saw as the efforts of feminists, Ruskin gave his well-known lecture "Of Queen's Garden" which was subsequently included in the volume *Sesame and Lilies* (1865). This is Millet's comment on this "refutation" (of feminist positions) by Ruskin: "his refutation is the courtly platitude that women are loved and honored, have nothing to complain of and are even treated as royalty, so long as they stay at home" (Vicinius 123).

Such elevation of the woman in the collective imaginary of the Victorians probably obscures the reality of domestic tyranny and cruelty of various kinds. In the words of Germaine Greer, the hearth, "the real theatre of the sex war despite the atrocities committed in social situations is the domestic hearth; *there* it is conducted unremittingly" (81). Her comment applies to instances where there is some fighting back, where there is resistance. But in many cases, especially in the Victorian era the oppression of woman by man went unresisted and uncontested. The novels of Dickens supply many glimpses of physical male tyranny. In *Little Dorrit* Flintwich giving his wife Affrey "such a dose" – pinching and squeezing her at will, and in *The Old Curiosity Shop* the frightening villain Quilp making his timid and good wife sit up the whole night, apart from subjecting her to other kinds of mental and physical torment – are but two of several examples. While these might be simply held up as examples of the Dickensian imagination which managed to give a dab of comicality to even the bleaker aspects of existence, it was undeniable that things were indeed not very cheery for women, whether of the lower or middle classes.

However, while instances in literary writings could be found about the victimhood or angelhood of women, there were also instances where strong, even demonic women were portrayed. While the dichotomous representation of women deserves some careful and separate attention through a reference to literary texts slightly later in this essay, it can be safely be asserted here that in the subconscious mind of the Victorians (some of whom were writers) a fear about rebellion in the family lurked, perhaps prompting them to give literary renderings of destructive womanhood. In the words of historian F. M. L. Thompson, "Many early Victorians supposed that they were witnessing a 'crisis of the family' that threatened, unless successfully tackled and resolved, to undermine the entire fabric of society and to sweep the nation into turbulent, uncharted, and perilous times of chaos and anarchy" (85). Such a fear never really disappears in the century. As Thompson somewhat dramatically goes on to put it, "Feminine rebellion against the duties and functions of childbearing and home-keeping seemed to be looming; and with the approaching collapse of parental, particularly paternal, authority, the end of the family as the basic unit of education and social training, or socialization, which transmitted all the habits and standards that enabled society to function, seemed to be in sight" (85). The portrayal of raging, violent, mad women such as Bertha in *Jane Eyre*, made famous by Susan Gilbert and Sandra Gilbert in the pioneering feminist work, *The Madwoman in the Attic* (1979), can be seen as instances of female rebellion erupting from prolonged subdual. Such representations of demoniacal energy represent the woman writer's own rage at being repressed rather than the fear and anxiety of male writers and male culture in general.

The point has been made that while fulfilment within the family was severely limited anyway, for some it was actually non-attainable because of the difficulties and often the near-impossibility of marrying and forming a family of one's own. There would be those late in the century, like Rhoda Fleming of Gissing's *The Odd Women*, who would boldly repudiate marriage. For those who yearned for marital and consequent familial fulfilment, the path was not smooth. In the writings of both male and female writers, the restricted, even claustrophobic existence of wives is frequently depicted. Anne Bronte draws on her own experience of living in close proximity to her brother Patrick Branwell Bronte and witnessing his slow but sure degradation, to create the character of Arthur Huntingdon in the novel *The Tenant of Wildfell Hall* (1848). For a long time Huntingdon's wife Helen Graham puts up with his adulterous flirtation with another woman, his drunken depravities, and his attempts to contaminate the mind of their son, but finally decides that she has had enough, and makes good her escape with the son. A relationship which is even more disturbing than the one between Arthur and Helen, indeed, one of the most vividly portrayed of troubled conjugal relationships one can see in the literature of the period, is the one between Grandcourt and Gwendolen in Eliot's *Daniel Deronda* (1876). Gwendolen is completely subjugated by the cold, tyrannical Grandcourt and allowed very little freedom although no material comfort is denied her.

In this and other works, one obvious basis for male supremacy is the financial clout enjoyed by men. Apart from the fact that women had hardly any choice of financially lucrative careers, various laws also prevented them from enjoying the money they could inherit from their fathers. This denial became particularly noticeable and unjust in the case of married women. The Matrimonial Causes Act of 1857 seemed a progressive measure as it became secularised with the settlements now taking place in the civil courts rather than in the ecclesiastical courts. This simplified matters for both parties and divorce was no longer a cumbersome, expensive and prolonged affair. (Under it, a Stephen Blackpool could have divorced his terrible wife, in *Hard Times.*) The Act also entailed payment of alimonies by a husband to a divorced or deserted wife. But the Act was still loaded against women and cried out for further reformative legislation. The bias of the legislation is seen from the fact that while the husband needed only to prove his wife's adultery, the wife had to prove her husband as being guilty of incest, bigamy, cruelty or desertion also, something which it was very difficult to do. Nevertheless, this Act was seen as marking some advance for women's condition in the realm of domesticity and civil society.

Before some of these new laws (for example, the First Married Women's Property Act of 1870 improved things further for women) came on the scene to ameliorate the lot of women, the supposition was rather sentimentally satisfying on the face of it: that the husband and wife were one. However, this bit of Victorian piety was hypocritical in its actual operation and even dangerous. What happened was that a woman actually surrendered her legal rights after marriage to the husband. The husband now held control over her property and income (in most cases inherited from a father or some rich relative). The Infant Custody Act gave women who were proven "innocent" in a divorce litigation the right to custody over their children.

The incongruence and injustice of a woman's material rights slipping out of her grasp after marriage is well brought out by John Stuart Mill:

> by means of settlements, the rich usually contrive to withdraw the whole or part of the inherited property of the wife from the absolute control of the husband: but they do not succeed in keeping it under her own control; the utmost they can do only prevents the husband from squandering it, at the same time debarring the rightful owner from its use . . . if he takes it [the property] from her by personal violence as soon as she receives it, he can neither be punished, nor compelled to restitution. (503–04)

After pointing out this in the instance of the nobler families, Mill sketches the disheartening scenario that prevails for the rest: "In the immense majority of cases there is no settlement: and the absorption of all rights, all property, as well as all freedom of action, is complete" (504). Finally Mill points out the real lacuna (which is a reflection of the notorious Victorian hypocrisy) that obtains in the legality of the thing: "The two are called 'one person in law', for the purpose of inferring that whatever is hers is his, but the parallel inference is never drawn that whatever is his is hers; the maxim is not applied against the man, except to make him responsible to third parties for her acts, as a master is for the acts of his slaves or of his cattle" (504). Such a lop-sided scenario hobbled a woman from conducting any meaningful business negotiations and thus made nonsense of her financial autonomy.

Given that the asymmetry in man–woman rights actually came to the fore as a result of a marital union, it is no wonder that many women – and a few male writers – subjected the issue of marriage to severe scrutiny. Perhaps reacting to the marriage convention which had acquired a semi-official status in the matter of applying closure in literary works, William Thackeray says:

> As his hero and heroine pass the matrimonial barrier, the novelist generally drops the curtain, as if the drama were over then: the doubts and struggles of life ended . . . . But our little Amelia was just on the bank of her new country, and was already looking anxiously back towards the sad friendly figures waving farewell to her across the stream, from the other distant shore. (303; ch. XXVI)

Amelia's foil in the novel –Becky – is sharp and calculating, but makes a wrong gamble and ends up marrying the proverbially penniless younger son Rawdon, when she could have got the *father*, Sir Pitt, had she perhaps been a little more patient. This is Thackeray's sly and insinuating comment on the situation: "If only people made prudent marriages, what a stop to population there would be!" (181; Ch. xvi). The fact is, nobody really makes imprudent marriages in the vanity fair or the marketplace that is the Victorian world in general. However, what the desperate aspirations and manoeuvres of Becky Sharp reveal is the financial insecurity of women. The penniless ones can hope for some rise in society by marrying into money. The ones that have money can hope to lose it to the least unworthy of men.

Women writers who tackle the subject of marriage (and it would be difficult to find one who does not at some point) sometimes look at it as ideal fulfilment. However, in many cases they seem more concerned to look at the impediments to a true and fulfilling union. That most romantic of novels, *Wuthering Heights*, charged up with the yearnings and energies of a set of lovers, ends with an ideal marriage that seems to signal future regeneration after protracted phases of strife and disharmony. But this happy marriage between Catherine the younger and Hareton Earnshaw cannot obscure the fact that the novel also mourns failed marriages and aborted romantic relationships. Before she marries the roughly reared but good and manly Hareton, Catherine the younger is forced by Heathcliff into a marriage with the sickly, self-pitying and selfish Linton Heathcliff, his own son. This marriage comes to an end with the death of Linton.

The most famous and compelling of the man–woman relationships in the novel is the one between Heathcliff and the older Catherine. Although both love each other with an other-worldly fervour, the relationship does not see fruition. Proper family values, so dear to the Victorians, do not materialise in the novel because the chief protagonists are denied conjugal fulfilment. Against the agonising fact of the two lovers tragically denied fulfilment in each other's arms, the final union between the two younger lovers struggles to posit a vision of enduring harmony and meaning. And why is it that the Heathcliff–Catherine union does not come about? It is because Catherine feels impelled to succumb to the pressures of marrying the "right" man, a man who will give her comfort and status, the kinds of things that Heathcliff the outcast from nowhere was not likely to. The realistic way in which Catherine describes her decision to throw in her lot with the well-to-do land-owning gentleman Edgar underscores a woman's predicament of not having much choice in the matter. To Nelly Dean's query about why she would not choose any handsome and rich young men other than Edgar, Catherine replies simply: "If there be any, they are out of my way: I have seen none like Edgar" (56; Ch. 9). It's true that the privileged, reasonably well-born Catherine is not as desperately constrained and bereft of options as the Madden sisters in Gissing's *The Odd Women,* but the phrase "out of my way" still indicates the limitations of women who were stuck in certain spaces and who could hardly venture out into the wider world to look for a worthy mate. Apart from the gender-induced limitations for a woman to roam about and look for fit marriage-partners, there is also the implicit, underlying limitation of a woman having no other way to fulfilment or social recognition except through marriage.

While Emily opts for a kind of romantic and defiant "solution" to such predicament by elevating the tragic separation of Heathcliff and Catherine above mortal and mundane marriages, with the hint that they enjoy an other-wordly union after all, her sister Charlotte Bronte – while not entirely eschewing the romantic credo – seems to explore the question of marriage and the related questions of man–woman relations and the nature of female identity in a somewhat more realistic way. As revealed by her letters, she also pondered deeply over the relevance of these issues in the real world. Aware of the reality of the "odd" or "superfluous" women for whom marriage might be a kind of mathematical or statistical impossibility given the lesser number of available men, she was resentful of the cultural imperative that assigned a central or definitive role to marriage in the lives of women. In her last novel *Villette*, Bronte explores the possibility of a woman leading an emancipated, independent single life in the career of Lucy Snowe. Lucy's lack of physical attractiveness seems to mark her out for a solitary destiny anyway. However, she does experience genuine love with Paul Emmanuel who appreciates her for the qualities of her mind. But it is suggested that Paul dies in a shipwreck although not before helping Lucy to set up a school of her own.

These lines capture very well the strange, haunting dichotomy of the lives of Victorian women. For the Victorians, the home was a shrine, and the wife (in her role of the wife or mother) was the presiding deity. But the remorseless imperatives of making a living often drew women far away from the home. In the case of working-class women such as Tess, the enforced distance between home and workplace was even greater. *Tess* is a late Victorian novel, but it is set in earlier times. The Industrial Revolution is in full swing. This phenomenon has had a big impact on family life. The natural contribution of women to home income now goes; it is all about wages and rates and professionalism. In some ways, women have retreated into the cocoon of the home. But this was not the case with all women. Some of them were compelled to engage with the dusty challenges of the workaday world to support their families. Such a one was Tess, who found herself cut off from the soothing confincs of family and loved ones precisely because that family was facing destitution and placing all the burdens of their upkeep on Tess's young shoulders.

The figure of Tess draws together many of the conflicts and challenges attendant on the existence of Victorian women that we have been discussing. Unlike Lucy Snowe of *Villette,* Tess is attractive, but that in itself is no guarantee that she was destined for a happy marriage. The question of gender often came yoked to the question of class. While the question of class with its link to the Industrial Revolution has already been dealt with, it can be pointed out here that in the case of a woman of a lower class, many of the problems that plagued women in general became more acute. Lack of money meant that they would not be shielded from the evils of the external world. Middle class and upper-class women may be pining for a life of genuine fulfilment not narrowly defined by the duties of being a caring mother and a gracious homemaker and hostess. Boredom and ennui might mark their lives. However, the lot of lower-class women was by no means enviable in this regard as Tess's experiences exemplify. She had to go out of her home to Trantbridge seeking charity at the hands of the richer relatives, the Durbeyfields. Her downfall occurs in the wide open spaces, far from the shelter of home. Alec "saves" her from a bunch of rowdy and hostile women, but leads her to a lonely spot and imposes himself sexually on her. As a result, she bears an illegitimate child which, apart from earning her opprobrium from her neighbours in her home village, damns any possibility of final happiness as her husband Angel is unable to bear the revelation about the encounter with Alec and its consequences.

Hardy's Tess is a central figure in feminist discussions about the role as well as the destiny of Victorian women. In her abbreviated but intense life, Hardy plays with many stock Victorian ideas and phenomena pertaining to women. Hardy's approach is often unconventional and even anti-patriarchal, although he too has been accused of male biases. One interesting thing is that he ironically uses the figure of the angel. Unlike many of his predecessors, he applies it to a man. Because Angel Clare fails to live up to the expectations of his name, religion is seen as inadequate in addressing the crises in the lives of common people. If anything, religion is actually seen as a persecuting force, as Tess is confronted with the scene of a man who paints messages from the Old Testament about adultery soon after she has had the sexual encounter with Alec.

The other idea that Hardy plays with and interrogates in an unconventional spirit, also not without religious implications, is that of the fallen woman. The idea of "fall" in the Christian context refers to the fall of both Adam and Eve: they were ejected from Paradise for disobediently eating the forbidden fruit. A special blame has always been attached to Eve because it was she who led Adam astray after being tempted by Satan in the form of a serpent. So it is that the "daughters of Eve" are always under suspicion. It is as if they are, on the one hand, sexual temptresses, luring men into moral pitfalls. On the other hand, they themselves are fragile, untrustworthy creatures, prone to succumbing to sexual temptations. In both cases, it is that original disobedience or lack of discipline that is their (and society's) bane. What makes things worse in Victorian culture is the heavy expectation from women to keep things pure and sanctified in a world seen increasingly as corrupt and complicated.

Mrs Grundy (who is an off-stage character in the 1798 play, *Speed the Plough* by Thomas Morton is known to make another character worry what she might say, and ever since then Grundy and Grundyism have become synonymous with rigid propriety and prudishness and an unofficial censoring of free speech) makes it difficult for the frank portrayal of sexual relations or acts. Victorian literature is more constrained and reticent in this regard in comparison to the eighteenth century where the novels of Smollett and Fielding often revel in situations of robust physical pleasures and carnality. The fact was that sexual activities, including the patronage of prostitutes, was not any the less subdued than in previous ages. It was rarely, however, that the Victorians could bring themselves to refer to sex. When fallen women *are* mentioned, the attitudes to such women who, in reality, provided clandestine pleasures to Victorian men, brings out the notorious Victorian double standard or hypocrisy which is reflected in various ways in the literature of the period and which Hardy was keen on combating at least in *Tess of the D'Urbervilles*.

The status of the women who pleasured men of all classes and dispositions was often pathetic and very vulnerable. Apart from the expected stigmatisation by society in general, the state also brought its heavy hand to bear on the lives of the sex workers. There were three Contagious Diseases Act – in 1864, 1866 and 1869, which were meant to control the spread of venereal diseases among the British soldiers through medical examinations of prostitutes. The implications were wider in a society which prided itself on its democratic and liberal temper. (There was actually a Liberal government in power at the time.) As Helen Rogers puts it, taking into account the resistance to these bills, "The defence of liberty underpinned opposition to the Acts: presumed guilty until she could prove her innocence and subject to imprisonment if she resisted treatment, the suspected woman was deprived of a fair trial and thus, it was claimed, the legislation overturned the fundamental principles of British law, threatening the rights and freedom of all" (125).

Before the acts were repealed after vigorous repeal movements led by contemporary feminists, many poor women faced humiliation and harassment at the hands of government inspectors and policemen especially because of the fact of the examination of their bodies. Due to the work by such activists, "sympathy shifted firmly away from men and towards women, even prostitutes, who were now viewed as the primary victims of State repression" (137). Whatever be the outcome of movements, it would have struck many sensitive people that the women were victims in more than one sense.

In the case of Tess, the sense of victimisation is more intense because of her poverty. It is also the case that there was very little room for women to completely recover from the consequences of a sexual encounter because of the strong cult of purity that obtained in Victorian times. Angels, after all, were the purest and most incorporeal of beings, and the ideal woman was an angelic being – a cultural consensus that resonates in a wide range of literary works. Hardy gives expression to his defiant stand in this matter by subtitling the work, "A Pure Woman", despite knowing that for most Victorians purity went no further than simply physical /sexual purity. He also has book headings such as "The Woman Pays" that brings home to one the Victorian double standard in the matter. (In *The Mayor of Casterbridge* too, men and women are partners in the sexual act, but the man is handicapped by this bit of shared scandal.) Not only is it that Alec faces no retribution for his "rape" of Tess, the more enlightened Angel also does not feel that his dalliance with a woman in London before his marriage with Tess need be placed on a comparable level to Tess's sexual experience. Tess is changed, but he remains the same. Similar is the case in George Eliot's *Adam Bede.* In this novel, the peasant girl Hetty Sorrel is seduced by the young squire Arthur Donnithorne. Hetty becomes pregnant but her world comes crashing down as she realises that Arthur has no intention of marrying her. She kills her newborn because she knows that there is no place in the world for such a child and that the existence of the baby will only mean her being branded as a fallen woman. However, her act is discovered and she is transported, just about escaping the fate of being hanged. Her lover Arthur knows genuine remorse, but society has no punishment for him. Both his class and gender come to his rescue.

The Victorians seemed utterly fascinated by the figure of the fallen woman. Probably influenced by the knowledge of a great number of prostitutes in their society, they did not confine themselves in their literature to the portrayal of only hardened professional and commercial prostitutes. Often they displayed an ambiguous penchant for women belonging to respectable backgrounds whom circumstances, or their own inner flaws, push into a state of fall. Sometimes the fallenness could simply be a form of sexual act outside the sanction of the married state, but at some other times it could be actual prostitution. While people like Hetty, Tess and Ruth belong to the former category, someone like Esther in *Mary Barton* falls into the latter category. Little Emily in *David Copperfield* is slightly more ambiguously portrayed (not untypically in Victorian literature where there is always some constraint in these matters), as it is implied that she was about to go into prostitution before she is rescued. Apart from dealing with the fates of major or important characters, the writers also give us glimpses of certain anonymous fallen women. Such is the case of the night creature who confronts Amy when the young heroine roams around all alone on the streets of London. While the portrayal of such characters is not without sympathy, there is still a warning to women embedded in such portrayals, by male and female writer alike. If women do not keep their sexuality firmly in control, or put themselves in situations where they might be pounced upon by predatory men, they risk being damned and cast away by society. Both the need to "punish" the fallen women, and the aversion to a frank depiction of sexual matters indicates Victorian culture's reluctance or inability to come to terms with women's sexuality.

Such a reluctance or inability is also seen in instances where the actual sexual act is out of sight. The angel icon whom we talked about in the beginning of the essay is one who has attained the blessed status of being otherworldly, by banishing improper thoughts from the minds of men. Characters like Agnes in *David Copperfield* and Sybil in Disraeli's novel of the same name may end up getting married, but it is their spirituality that defines their position in the narratives. Symbolising the role of the good angel from the moment she appears, acting as a soothing domestic caregiver for both father and David, Agnes's function in the narrative is hardly at the bodily level. Her domestic chores are as a matter of course and to be taken for granted and not really worth mention: what is more important is what she contributes to David's spiritual progress.

Agnes is, of course, not central to the narrative but the titular heroine of the work *Sybil* is. A greater burden is placed on her shoulders as the canvas here is broader and the issues of greater public urgency than what we see in Dickens's novel.

Industrial unrest rages in the novel and opposing sides seem locked into implacably antagonistic postures. What seems to be needed is the healing touch of an angelic woman rather than intricate negotiations between leading representatives of the Rich and the Poor. This Sybil provides, exuding a saintly aura throughout and behaving like a merciful sister of charity. At one point in the novel where Sybil pacifies a crying child in a poor working-class household, the mother exclaims: "You are an angel from heaven!" (120) She is unwittingly summing up the role that seems to have been assigned to Sybil in the work. Finally, like many Victorian domestic angels Sybil is made to enter the human, material sphere through marriage which is almost jarring since so insistent has been her spiritual or saintly identity. This is, however, a symbolic marriage, meant to unite the warring factions of the aristocrats and the proletariats. Referring to the observations of contemporary reviewers, Sheila M. Smith says: "the plot does *not* unite the 'Two Nations'. Sybil is not a daughter of the people, who, we are told, are not worthy to provide a husband for her, but an aristocrat in disguise . . . Its [the novel's] vision does not spring from its factual observations, but is rather imposed upon them" (xvi). This cosmetic nature of the novelistic vision is particularly visible in the way women like Sybil are made to play the roles of domestic angels.

Very often such definition also attains greater moral clarity through a positioning against a dark, devil woman although in rare cases we see the female angel morally pitted against a male devil: apart from the example of *David Copperfield* already cited, we can also give the instance of Dickens's *Little Dorrit* where the virtuous and angelic Amy Dorrit is seen in a moment of physical juxtaposition with the fiendish French intriguer Blandois-Rigaud. But the angel-demon opposition is more compelling when two women are concerned. It seems that the Victorians are willing to elevate women to a pedestal, but the least sign of transgression or improper behaviour will make them come crashing down. The angel becomes a fallen angel which is an interesting cultural take on the figure of the fallen woman. In such cases the sexuality seems repressed and is manifested through other forms of depravity or bad behaviour.

William Thackeray and Anthony Trollope seem to mock the Victorian tendency to play off fair, angelic women against dark, satanic ones. These two writers seem much less committed to the domestic or family idyll where the wife/mother is content to play the ministering angel at home. They also comically exploit the Victorian need for social stability that requires the submission or subordination of women within the familial context. The importance of the family, touched on in the beginning of this chapter, is highlighted by Nancy Armstrong in her discussion of *Vanity Fair* which has the panoramic Napoleonic Wars as the backcloth: "Thackeray's concern for Napoleonic history notwithstanding, the author's perspective in *Vanity Fair* is certainly neither on the grand scope of political events in Europe nor on the fortunes of men in love and war. His is the record of the small shock waves felt on the homefront by two women who endeavour to keep themselves well-supported by men" (44). The two women in question here are the fair, innocent Amelia and the "dark", scheming Becky Sharp. Amelia dreams of nothing beyond setting up a home with George Osborne. Becky too wants a marriage, and gets it too, but for her all powerful men are prospective prey.

Becky is a figure from nowhere – no proper home, no family reputation. Her "homelessness" endows her with a rage that fuels the energies of the narrative. Like Satan, she allures and tempts both men and women to their downfall. She is compared to a marine cannibal because of her rapacious desires. However, the angel-demoness antithesis is not sustained by Thackeray. Despite her negative role, Becky hardly does any more damage to society than Amy. In fact, she actually succeeds in exposing the hollow pretensions of upper-class society. The angelic Amy, on the other hand, is a parasitic creature who does little except dote on her husband (whose vanity she feeds) and then after his death, on her son. In the words of Roger Henkle, Becky's "comic freedom and exploitation of sterile social fictions must apparently be curtailed because of her author's reluctance, finally, to renounce social order" (18).

The demon figure in *Barchester Towers* is Madeline Neroni, who has eyes "as bright as Lucifer's" (67; Bk 1, 9). An exotic "outsider," she is regarded with fear and loathing by many characters in the centre of the social scene. The Evangelist Slope seems to fall under her spell for a while. However, Madeline seems to support the party opposed to him because of which Slope thinks of her as a devil-figure: "Whenever he again thought of her in his dreams, it was not as of an angel with azure wings. He connected her rather with fire and brimstone, and though he could still believe her to be a spirit, he banished her entirely out of heaven, and found a place for her among the infernal gods" (448; Bk 3, Ch. 12). The mock-heroic thrust of the language is a clear indication that Trollope is not going along here with the simplistic angel-demon applied to women. This is because the angel in the house here, Eleanor Bold, is like Amy a parasitic creature, while the Satanic temptress Madeline does more to help people than Eleanor.

As Armstrong says, the family is certainly very important and often plays a larger role in the narrative dynamics than the bigger events which sometimes frame the main action. However, very often, both male and female writers often sabotage Victorian familial norms even when they centralise the family or domesticity in their works, as we have seen in the case of Thackeray and Trollope. Many male writers also showed more overt sympathy for the plight of women, although unlike someone like the utilitarian philosopher John Stuart Mill who strenuously argued for a better dispensation for women, the fiction writers were not always consistent.

While imaginatively empowering women to a point, they felt the need to tame the aspirations of women. Thus Thackeray and Trollope celebrate the powers of Becky and Madeline, but then finally clip their wings or make them depart from the social scene. Thomas Hardy not only creates lifelike and likable heroines such as Tess and Marty (in *The Woodlanders*, 1887), but also mounts a critique of society that is dependent on the adoption of a female perspective. Yet, he also leaves us with a strong sense that women will tempt men and lead them astray or betray them at crucial junctures. This seems to be the case certainly, in *Jude the Obscure* (with Arabella and Sue both contributing to his downfall in their own ways) and to an extent even in *Far from the Madding Crowd* (1874) and *The Mayor of Casterbridge*. In *Return of the Native* (1878) he seems to be concerned to present the dangers of all-consuming, heedless female desire in the figure of Eustacia Vye.

It was difficult for male writers to transcend prevailing notions about gender. However, at this juncture it may be well to point out that the stance of male writers is not always necessarily one of condescending or heartfelt sympathy or barely disguised hostility. In a book called *Male Writers and Female Masquerade*, Anne Robinson Taylor sketches a more complex thesis. She makes the interesting argument that a host of famous male writers actually borrowed from the arsenal of womanly emotions as they in their maleness were culturally constrained. By identifying with their female characters, they could explore emotions that they were otherwise denied access to.

Nevertheless, in an age of scientific enquiries and commercial expansion, women remained objects rather than subjects. The oft-repeated phrase "commodification of women" had a special resonance in Victorian times. Lacking will, initiative or agency, they were items, pawns, commodities, to be tinkered with, manipulated, slotted, and also represented in ways that re-affirmed their "object" status. Often a woman's attractiveness was enhanced by her financial status. Victorian literature is full of instances where a woman's stock rises when she is found to be an heiress or has substantial properties or wealth to her name. This is how the character Lord George Carruther persuades himself to have a favourable view of the scheming and heartless but rich Lizzie Eustace in *The Eustace Diamonds*: ". . . he *told* himself that she was wondrous pretty. And then her pluck was so good! And she had four thousand a year!" (352, Bk 1, Ch. 38). As for the good Lucy, this is the assessment that Mrs Greystock, thinking about the marriage of her son Frank, is compelled to come up with: "There was no doubt about Lucy being as good as gold; – only that real gold, vile as it is, was the one thing that Frank so much needed" (276; Bk 1, Ch. xxxx). In *The Mayor of Casterbridge*, Lucetta suddenly becomes attractive in the eyes of both Henchard and Donald Farfrae because she is an heiress. Social morality itself is subordinate to the subject of private finances. However, there is irony in the fact that even rich women found it difficult to manage their own finances because of legal and social issues. One of the reasons why they became attractive was that their chosen men would have a claim on their wealth after marriage, as already seen above.

The love triad of Lucetta–Henchard–Donald is also clearly Darwinian. While the basic Darwinian situation is that the female chooses between two competing males, in real life she was more prize to be won than a creature with very active powers of choice. Actually, like the world of finance, both science and religion could be seen as keeping women in a state of stasis or subjugation. Religion made unreal demands, expecting women to diffuse through society a symbolic radiance by effacing themselves or playing the roles of succouring figures at death beds etc. Science proceeded on the basis of a more diminished view of the nature of woman. In the age of evolutionary paradigms, women seemed somehow to be lagging behind, due to inherent inferiorities. As Patricia Murphy points out, women's intuitive capacities as against the capacity to rationally reflect on events, was praised. This was really a case of damning with faint praise and reflected an attitude that consigned women to a lower state of development. She goes on to say: "Scientists tended to compare women's mental capacities to those of children as well as 'lower civilizations' or 'savages.' Underlying such comparisons was the supposition that men held the highest position in evolutionary development, with women invariably positioned below" (25).

Many men of the period could be seen to be harbouring "a strictly scientific view of women" like Lydgate in *Middlemarch,* who had recoiled from a woman who had baffled him with her bizarre behaviour. This same novel, which balances the quest for scientific certainties against the customary weight of "opinions" (the novel abounds in words like "opinions" and "views"), has statements like the following about women: "Women were expected to have weak opinions" (31; Bk 1, Ch. 1). Also, women are linked with the (trivial) arts rather than with the rigours of commerce or science. As Mr Brooke says patronisingly: "But there is a lightness about the feminine mind – a touch and go – music, the fine arts, that kind of thing . . . A woman should be able to sit down and play you or sing you a good old English tune" (89; Bk 1, Ch. 7).

The author of all these, George Eliot herself is a shining example of the way certain women rose above prevailing notions about the nature and potentialities of women. The most scientific personality in *Middlemarch* is Eliot herself. In her avatar of the third person omniscient narrator, Eliot is realistic and analytical, not intuitive and temperamental. In her ability to comprehend and communicate various scientific paradigms of the century, including that of the evolutionary doctrine, she gives the lie to stereotypical notions about the nature of women that Murphy mentions.

When talking about the position of women vis-à-vis the family in particular and the community in general, one need not dwell only on the negative aspects. The women of the Victorian period definitely made significant strides, and the positive developments sometimes find an echo in the literature of the period. Many women's movements took roots during the period in response to the iniquities unleashed on women. The repeal of the Contagious Acts movement burgeoned and energised the cause of the suffragists and others. Female occupations also diversified. One of the more significant developments of Victorian culture was the coming-into-being of the New Woman. First coined by writer Sarah Grand, this figure captured the imagination of writers and thinkers. The New Woman was radically different from the Angel in the House. Clearly she had benefited from the various legislations about property as well as from the fact of different educational portals opening up for women.

The New Woman breaks away from the moulds set or sanctioned by society. In many ways a real-enough figure – she was a result of various drives and movements for women's emancipation in different spheres of society – this entity was also a discursive or literary construct. As a new *kind* of woman started to emerge in the 1880s and 90s with striking credentials such as educational degrees, work experience and accomplishments, and above all, a resistant attitude to time-hallowed social ideals such as marriage and motherhood, the creative mind also responded to the phenomenon, thus playing its part in the creation of the New Woman.

Marriage was never a readily available option for Victorian women, as already shown. But the New Woman deliberately rejects this possibility, exercising her right to *choose* not to marry. At the same time, however, they asserted sexual freedom. This was not easy or simple, considering how hidebound and prejudiced Victorian society was in this matter. The women themselves had internalised societal conventions. At the same time, when we look at the attitudes of various literary characters in late Victorian fiction, as well as attitudes towards them, it is clear that something new is happening here. Earlier, the angelic, pure, somewhat other-worldly maiden and the comfortable, matronly, motherly type had divided the territory between them, with a few complex, atypical figures thrown in. Now appears a woman who is actually difficult to categorise, as in the following description of militant feminist Rhoda Nunn in *The Odd Women*:

> Self-confidence, intellectual keenness, a bright humour, frank courage, were traits legible enough; and when the lips parted to show their warmth, their fullness, when the eyelids drooped a little in meditation, one became aware of a suggestiveness directed not solely to the intellect, of something like *an unfamiliar sexual type* [emphasis mine] remote indeed from the voluptuous, but hinting a possibility of subtle feminine forces that might be released by circumstances. (22; Ch. 3)

According to Elaine Showalter, "The 1890s, Gissing believed, were a period of necessary 'sexual anarchy,' during which the feminist campaigns of the New Women challenged the most deeply held attitudes and ideologies of the culture" (vii). This "sexual anarchy," Showalter goes on to add, is simply, "the questioning of gender roles during the 1890s" (vii).

It seems that through the portrayal of Rhoda Nunn, George Gissing is trying to break the stereotype of the conventional Victorian heroine. She represents a strong possibility for full emancipation or redemption for women, after decades of nullity or futility. Not tied down by sentimental attachment to anything or anyone, to any sugary ideals of domesticity or romance in particular, she boldly charts her own path and is willing to lend a hand to any like-minded woman. It is not as if she is sexually frigid either, although there is an ambiguous play on her last name, with Nunn being suggestive of *nun*. She seems to be attracted to the liberal-minded Everett, brother of her activist friend Mary Barfoot. However, she repudiates the options of romance or domesticity by refusing to link her lot with Everett's.

Despite the vision of a hopeful future (almost the last words of the novel are "The world is moving!"), this is, however, a realistic order created by a writer known for the drab, depressing colours in which he paints his world full of floundering, derelict souls. Gissing was influenced by the movement of naturalism, which focused on the harsh and sordid circumstances of life. The world that Gissing wrote about was not yet blooming with possibilities for women. In keeping with this, in this novel we have a series of drooping, defeated women to set against the vigour and optimism of women such as Rhoda Nunn and Mary Barfoot. The New Woman is then no sentimental distortion of reality even if an emancipatory attitude may lie behind it. Actually, some of the situations and characters depicted in *The Odd Women* were probably prevalent in the worlds that earlier Victorians wrote about, too. Only, except for those odd moments when a writer's fancy was captured by the dramatic possibilities of the destiny of a fallen woman, Victorian fiction seemed to paper over much of the depressing or uncomfortable facts of life.

"New Woman" literature often makes the lessons of some of the sobering data about the unpromising fates of most women more explicit. It can be seen as the logical culmination of the development of the novel that centres the Woman Question. With modern questions about the purpose of life taking over, and modernity itself becoming a brooding fact of life, women's roles had to be seen in more original ways, befitting the changed and changing times. With religious faith seriously undermined and Social Darwinism getting a grip on the minds of people, women could no longer be seen as aloof from the struggle for existence. A protective, sheltering view towards women is held only by the naive and the foolish guardians of an outmoded paternalism: "Let men grapple with the world . . . I should grieve indeed if I thought my girls would ever have to distress themselves about money matters" (1; Ch. 1). The speaker is Dr Madden, a man who has sheltered his daughters from the world, and thus leaves them unfit for its struggles when he dies prematurely.

While life is testing and often unyielding, new careers and options are also opening up. It could be just be the career of a typist or a secretary, but the old attitudes that liked to see women as part almost of the household furniture or as tender flowers that would wilt in the heat and strife of existence is largely gone. The New Woman is definitely a product of the new atmosphere, benefiting from developments in the modern world relating to education and career prospects.

Sue Bridehead in Hardy's last novel *Jude the Obscure* is a good example of the New Woman in literature. She is a bit of an intellectual and is well-educated. More strikingly, she is sexually liberated, choosing to live out of wedlock. While Sue is the closest approximation to the figure of the New Woman in Hardy's fiction, Tess also has something of the New Woman about her. Her education, her ambition and more modern attitudes mark her off from her mother's generation.

Perhaps in keeping with the still grim realities that characterise the lives of many women of the period, New Woman literature often comes off as less than triumphant or celebratory in tone. The heyday of the New Woman was in the closing two decades of the nineteenth century, a time when complete emancipation was still some distance away and could only dimly be apprehended. The vote and many other rights and safeguards for women lay in the future.

The stories of the New Woman then, not surprisingly, do not climax in unqualified happiness. The independent young woman who promised much with her bold and progressive ways lapsing into conformity or meeting with a tragic end formed something of a pattern. As Cedric Watts notes, except a few instances such as Vivie Warren in *Mrs Warren's Profession,* " . . . the New Woman's revolt ends either tragically or in conformity. Herminia, the heroine of *The Woman Who Did,* eventually commits suicide; the 'Gypsy' of *Keynotes* succumbs to the claims of maternity; Evadne, in *The Heavenly Twins,* emerges from a mental breakdown to acquiesce in a second marriage and motherhood" (154). Such setbacks may reflect the writers' realistic and even cynical awareness that the world was not yet ready to completely unfetter women. Where the male writers were concerned, the defeat of the New Woman may indicate an unconscious reluctance to fully accept the autonomy of women.

Sue's sad history is another case in point, particularly interesting because unlike most of the other writers mentioned by Watts, Hardy was a major writer. This most promising and radical of the New Woman figures finally treads the disheartening path of conformity. As her eldest child Father Time kills his siblings, Sue feels that she has been punished for her sinful ways. As for Tess, her journey towards emancipation does not go very far because the man she falls in love with turns out to be a slave of conformity after all, unable to adopt a sexually progressive attitude regarding the disclosure about her sexual liaison with another man. Yet another of Hardy's heroines, Elizabeth Jane, who shows herself to be a New Woman-like figure with her intense desire to improve herself intellectually, also finds true emancipation or happiness eluding her.

While the New Woman is thus depicted in a realistic and even underwhelming fashion at times – which is a reflection of contemporary sociological realties as the writers perceived them, it is undeniable that the late-Victorian ideal of the New Woman lights up the literary scene, energising the creative imagination. From Hardy's tragic Sue and Tess to Meredith's witty and spirited heroines such as Clara (a witty and resilient woman who gets the better of the formidable but hollow and insecure male tyrant Willoughby Patterne in the novel *The Egoist* [1879] and Diana Warwick in *Diana of the Crossways* [1885]), what we have is a gallery of credible, complex-minded women. This is an advance on the doll-like, Madonna figures who were the staple heroines of many works of early and mid-Victorian literature.

As far as the *real* future of women was concerned, energetic writings by sympathetic male thinkers such as John Stuart Mill as well as by women such as Harriet Martineau paved the path for equality, liberty, and emancipation. Activism over issues such as the unfair and anomalous Contagious Diseases Acts, the contested rights to property and to divorce and the denial of educational and voting rights provided a fillip to the feminist movement. As Janaki Nair points out, women were entering the public domain, and "by their alliances with the growing socialist and labour movement, women, too joined the ranks of the dangerous classes" (233). Which is to say, the establishment could no longer ignore, oppress or patronise them; rather, it had reason to fear their power. The peals and thunders of suffragism inspirited women and women writers, although the vote would only be granted in 1918, and that also only to women over thirty who were householders or married to householders. The angel in the house was by then seen regularly in the streets or other external spaces.

Works Cited

Armstrong, Nancy. *Desire and Domestic Fiction. A Political History of the Novel.* Oxford: Oxford UP, 1987. Print.

Bronte, Charlotte. *Shirley*. London: Penguin Books, 2012. Print. The Penguin English Library.

———. *Villette*. London and Melbourne: J. M. Dent, 1983. Print. Everyman's Library.

Brontë, Emily. *Wuthering Heights*. Ware, Hertfordshire: Wordsworth Editions Limited, 1992. Print. Wordsworth Classics.

Davidoff, Leonore and Catherine Hall. *Family Fortunes: Men and Women of the English Middle Class, 1780–1850*. London and New York: Routledge, 1987. Print.

Dickens, Charles. *David Copperfield*. Harmondsworth, Middlesex, England: Penguin Books, 1966. Print. The Penguin English Library.

Ellis, Sarah Stickney. *The Women of England: Their Social Duties, and Domestic Habits*. New York: D. Appleton & Co., 1839. Print.

Eliot, George. *Middlemarch*. Harmondsworth, Middlesex, England: Penguin Books, 1983. Print. Penguin Classics.

Gaskell, Elizabeth. *The Life of Charlotte Bronte*. London and Melbourne: J. M. Dent, 1984. Print. Everyman's Library.

———. *Ruth*. Chapman and Hall, 1853. Kindle.

Gissing, George. *The Odd Women*. London: Penguin Books, 1993. Print. Penguin Classics.

Greer, Germaine. *The Female Eunuch*. London: Paladin, 1970. Print.

Hardy, Thomas. *Tess of the D'Urbervilles*. New Delhi: Oxford UP, 2005. Print. Oxford World's Classics.

———. *Jude the Obscure*. Harmondsworth, Middlesex, England: Penguin Books. Print. Penguin Classics.

Henkle, Roger. *Comedy and Culture: England 1820–1900*. Princeton: Princeton UP, 1980. Print.

Mill, John Stuart. *The Subjection of Women. On Liberty and Other Essays*. Oxford: Oxford UP, 1991. Print. The World's Classics.

Millet, Kate. "The Debate over Women: Ruskin vs. Mill." *Suffer and Be Still: Women in the Victorian Age*. Ed. Martha Vicinius. Bloomington and Indianapolis: Indiana UP, 1973. 121–39. Print.

Murphy, Patricia. *In Science's Shadow: Literary Constructions of Late Victorian Women.* Columbia and London: U of Missouri P, 2006. Print.

Nair, Janaki. "Uncovering the *Zenana:* Visions of Indian Womanhood in English Women's Writings, 1813–1940." Catherine Hall, ed. *Cultures of Empire: Colonizers in Britain and the Empire in the Nineteenth and Twentieth Centuries: A Reader.* Manchester: Manchester UP, 2000. 224–45. Print.

Patmore, Coventry. *Angel in the House.* Web. Project Gutenberg. 14 March 2015. <http://www.gutenberg.org/ebooks>.

Peterson, M. Jeanne. "The Victorian Governess: Status Incongruence in Family and Society. Vicinius. 3–19.

Rogers, Helen. "Women and Liberty." *Liberty and Authority in Victorian Britain.* Ed. Peter Mandler. Oxford: Oxford UP, 2006. 125–55. Print.

Showalter, Elaine. "Introduction." Gissing, *The Odd Women.* vii–xxvi. Print.

Smith, Sheila M. "Introduction." Disraeli, *Sybil OR The Two Nations.* Oxford: Oxford UP, 2008. vii–xvii. Print. Oxford World's Classics.

Strachey, Lytton. "Florence Nightingale." *Eminent Victorians.* Radford VA: Wilder Publications, 2008. 84–125. Print.

Thackeray, William Makepeace. *Vanity Fair.* New York: Signet Books, 1982. Print.

Thompson, F. M. L. *The Rise of Respectable Society: A Social History of Victorian Britain: 1830–1900.* Cambridge, Mass.: Harvard UP, 1988. Print.

Trollope, Anthony. *The Eustace Diamonds.* Oxford: Oxford UP, 1983. Print. The World's Classics.

Watts, Cedric. "Hardy's Sue Bridehead and the 'New Woman.'" *Critical Survey,* 5.2 (1993): 152–56. Web. 14 May 2015.

SIX

Education in Victorian England

Education may appear to be a lesser subject in comparison to others, and the context of education not comparable to various social, political, and historical contexts when one studies the conditions of the production and consumption of works of Victorian literature. The daily routines, deeds and even the trials and ordeals of schoolboys surely cannot have the same resonance or repercussion as the questions of heaven and hell, the "descent" of man from the ape or other creatures, the Industrial Revolution and international trade and commerce, the planting of the Union Jack in far-flung corners of the globe, or the agonising questions of women's rights and identities. However, the fact remains that for generations of readers world-wide, it is the pictures of school-life depicted in novels such as *Nicholas Nickleby*, *David Copperfield*, *Jane Eyre*, and to a lesser extent, in *Tom Brown's School Days*, that remain some of the most unforgettable and enduring moments of Victorian literature.

Actually, like all the other concerns I have been addressing in this book, education also derives its importance from being interlinked with other aspects of life. For instance, education was part of the religious dispensation in many ways. While the instruction provided in England's schools and universities was no longer exclusively or predominantly theological as in earlier ages, religious and moral teaching was still insisted upon within educational premises. The great universities Oxford and

Cambridge were closed to Nonconformists and Catholics for some part of the century before reform took over.

At the same time, the sciences were also infiltrating into curriculums. When one tackles the subject of science in its totality, how it was taught and disseminated is also of importance, not just what was done and discovered in laboratories, or expeditions to remote locations on the ever-expanding globe. As for the question of women's rights and education, the walls of academia were some of the last barricades that remained to be breached, apart of course, from the subject of voting rights. In some ways, the most interesting, if not the most obvious, relationship is the one between education and imperialism or colonialism. While different pedagogical strategies were at work in the educational system, and while various moral and practical goals were contemplated and debated, one of the great aims of educational policy (especially in the public schools), was to equip young Englishmen to serve in the various towns and outposts of the British empire abroad. The interface between education and all these other aspects provide fruitful scope for the student of Victorian literature to engage with.

In works of literature, the theme of education is interestingly tied up with other pervasive Victorian preoccupations. Education lends its metaphors and images to many Victorian narratives, and sometimes the specificity of educational practices – good and bad, solemn and ludicrous – underscores the importance of education for the creative imagination. Many Victorian novels are indeed narratives of education. The protagonists of works as diverse as *David Copperfield, Great Expectations, The Adventures of Harry Richmond* (1871), *The Ordeal of Richard Feverel, Vanity Fair, The History of Henry Esmond* (1852), *Jane Eyre* and *The Mill on the Floss* educate themselves or are educated by others in both a specific and a general sense. These are bildungsromane, novels of growth: a greatly popular sub-genre of Victorian literature. Just as a student struggles through a difficult curriculum in school, the protagonists of these works face the challenges of the curriculum of life itself. He or she progresses, matures, evolves, and sometimes fails to do so, as if failing the test of life. All the time, the shadow of the Victorian imperative of *progress* hovers above the protagonist's endeavours, testing, trying, extracting the best out of him and her. The Victorians' obsession with progress in all spheres including education had a strongly materialistic base, but this was also reflective of their belief about the transformable quality of human life which was a little different from the more static views of human nature that prevailed in the eighteenth century. And education was one thing that in an increasingly democratic age would be able to transform one's fortunes and even one's personality.

The public school is certainly a very striking and central symbol, not just of British education in the usual sense but of the nation's attempts to construct a certain way of life that could become a tool for world dominance. Some of the great public schools were: Eton, Rugby, Harrow, Winchester, and Shrewsbury. It was said that the battle of Waterloo was won on the playing fields of Eton, and the empire too.

The education of the young was a particularly compelling subject. The cult of the child, a Romantic legacy, continued to fascinate people well into the Victorian period. The world of the child was one that offered symbolic suggestions: it was a cradle of present innocence and a stage for future growth. There is no dearth of poems or stories testifying to the often symbolic and spiritual role that children were burdened with in Victorian literature. Another reason why school education was on the forefront of public consciousness as compared to college education had to do with numbers or quantities. After all, at any given point of time, there were always many more school children than there were college-going or university-going young adults. Parents did not often feel the need or pressure to think of college or university education for their children, but some form of school education was deemed a necessity, especially for boys.

The interest in formal school education was sometimes paralleled by an interest in the subject of education imparted outside the boundaries of state or privately run institutions of learning. In the didactic Victorian age, the instillation of different social and ethical values into young minds being regarded as important, it was felt that disciplining and some amount of actual textbook teaching could be done at home. This was also connected to the great emphasis placed on family life, an emphasis which would decline in the next century. Of course, "values" also had a commercial undertow, however camouflaged it might be by high-minded rhetoric about the noble mission of education. Igor Webb poses the following questions in a chapter on production of value, education and character (Elsewhere in the study he shows how "value" or someone's sense of worth figures in human, romantic relationships too.): "What are the sources of real value in this changing society? How can value be effectively produced (or reproduced) – that is, what sort of education will create 'good' people? Has the older generation met its responsibility for educating the younger?" (47).

These questions are interesting in a book that deals with the industrial revolution and the novel. In an age heavily under the influence of utilitarianism and the laissez-faire philosophy, it is inevitable that education would be measured and weighed for the benefits it imparts to both individual and the community. However, other things are involved when one talks about the responsibility of the older generation towards the younger in the matter of education.

Sometimes, the older generation was a little over-zealous in imposing its educational ideology on the younger generation. Writers as diverse in aim and achievement as Charles Dickens and Thomas Hughes felt the injustice of heavy-handedly making children go through educational labours. These two writers wished to stress freedom and the joy of living above everything else, whether it be in the home or in places of learning. While teaching moral values through education pre-dated the Victorians and continues to be a potent item on the agendas of many educationists even today, Dickens had a real problem with this. "Moral" belonged to the arsenal of the orthodox who suffocated children with doctrinal matters. "Values," on the other hand, was an ambiguous term which could easily be appropriated by the utilitarians, also to suffocate the children and turn their lives into dreary wastelands.

But Dickens would have no quarrel with the contention that certain qualities could be nurtured in the family itself. While the Victorian family had not been always a bower of bliss, there was in fact something like a consensus that the first educational moves to train a child to become a worthy member of society would take place within family confines. Activist–writer Harriet Martineau in the revealingly titled *Household Education* (1849) often waxes moral while talking about the importance of the lessons that are to be given to the child in early life. Perhaps she sensed and anticipated the impending urbanisation of life and the coming shadow of split, modern existence and thus felt the need for the healing touch of homely nurturing. Towards the very beginning of the book she stresses a kind of family unity or cohesion: "Every member of the family above the yearling infant must be a member of the domestic school of mutual instruction . . . ." While she addresses the question in a very broad way (she talks, for example, of older people also having the capacity to learn), she is consistent in her emphasis on home life as a crucial educational instrument: "Every home being a school for old and young together, it is necessary, if the training is to be a good one, to be clear as to what the schooling is for. . . (Ch. V). "There is no occasion to point out here how great are the moral advantages of a good home in comparison with the best of schools," she further says.

Martineau may seem somewhat conventional and moralistic in some of her utterances, but she has things to say which would be regarded as progressive by any standard. Particularly noteworthy are her remarks about the victims of the paternalistic educational agenda: women and children. While her assertions about the compelling necessity of women's education will be treated later in this chapter, her remarks about the right way to go about "educating" the child bears mention here. In the matter of treating the child with compassion, Martineau is quite like Dickens. The moralistic or Evangelical zeal on the one hand, and the aspirational and calculating utilitarian spirit on the other had ensured that many children's lives had become gloomy and joyless. If schools were strict, home discipline often matched the stern, exacting routines of school. While stressing that children should not be indulged, Martineau also insists that their wills should not be broken. She also underlines the necessity of reading good fiction as conducive to the proper growth of mind.

In matters such as allowing the child the necessary imaginative space to grow freely, the stoutest champion of child rights is Charles Dickens. Echoing Martineau's words about allowing the child to read good fiction but making this an even more pivotal matter, Dickens shows how mental growth is stunted and twisted when the child is denied the pleasures of reading fairy-tales. Thus, in *Hard Times* Louisa and Tom, the children of the utilitarian schoolmaster Gradgrind, are sullen and repressed, veritable misfits of society. Gradgrind keeps his children away from nursery rhymes, jingles and fairy tales:

> No little Gradgrind had ever learnt the silly jingle, Twinkle, twinkle little star; how I wonder what you are! No little Gradgrind had ever known wonder on the subject, each little Gradgrind having at five years old dissected the Great Bear like a Professor Owen, and driven Charles Wain like a locomotive engine-driver. (11–12; Bk 1, Ch. 3)

Gradgrind enforces the same arid, unimaginative scheme while dealing with the students in his school, making them cram facts and figures like automatons. The obsessively fact-based educational regime here is the result of the mindless incorporation of the utilitarian philosophy with its essentially economic premise. Because this philosophy did not pay enough heed to the elusive imponderables of human nature, Dickens found it unacceptable. Facts and pre-determined theories were particularly unsuitable for the full and free growth of the child's mind, he felt.

While Dickens was a reformer himself, the utilitarian brand of education was also reformist in its ambition as it tried to address the issue of universal education. Too many children in Victorian society were missing the benefits of education, it was felt. Reformers also believed that education would contribute to the welfare and progress of the nation. The different Reform Acts of the century were widening the electoral base, and with the working-classes getting the vote, it was important to educate them and their children to make the purpose of electoral reform more meaningful.

Paul Schlicke in his Introduction to *Hard Times* points out:

> Under the guidance of Poor Law Assistant Commissioner James Kay-Shuttleworth, the monumentally important minute of 1846 had set up a teacher-training programme devised to improve educational standards by rapidly producing a large number of qualified instructors . . . The Minute created a pupil-teacher scheme to expand college training of teachers; and it awarded scholarships, based on examination results, to encourage further study by the ablest pupil-teachers. (xii)

Discussing the history of one such training college, Kneller Hall (instituted to address hereditary pauperism by weaning children from vagrancy and destitution through education), and in particular the fates of pupil-teachers, Christopher Bischoff says, however, that "the overall story of Kneller Hill reveals the difficulty Victorian reformers encountered in attempting to implement professional reform by well-paid, zealous agents of the state working nine-to-five performing a specific task" (1041). These teachers, who were supposed to embody the greatly popular ideal of masculinity for their Poor House students, found their career rather unrewarding as also effeminate (since they had to wash the floor and perform other such related chores).

These are some instances where a broad, universalistic intervention seemed to fail in Victorian Britain due to certain internal flaws and external obstacles. However, whether one is talking about the real-life James Kay-Shuttleworth or the fictional Thomas Gradgrind, the intention at least is good and honest. What about cases where the intent was bad to begin with?

There were many instances where a combination of harmful intent and rank pedagogical inability turned education into a nightmare scenario. In *Hard Times*, the damage is done mainly to the spirit (that is, of course, bad enough) and there is no evidence of the infliction of crude, corporal punishment on the students or the Gradgrind children. For someone like Gradgrind, repentance is a possibility, although by the time he repents, it is too late for his own children. But at least the suggestion is made that if an educator is made to see the error of his ways, reform is possible and there is some hope. There are other representatives of education in the fiction of Dickens who inflict harm on both the body and spirit of children. *David Copperfield* is an autobiographical novel which builds on many of Dickens's childhood experiences, including stints under despised teachers and headmasters. We meet here the cruel and tyrannical Creakle, about whom the young David heard that "Mr Creakle had not preferred his claim to being a Tartar without reason; that he was the sternest and most severe of masters; that he laid about him, right and left, every day of his life, charging in among the boys like a trooper, and slashing away, unmercifully" (138; Ch. 6).

It turns out that his reputation is not undeserved. He inflicts a particularly humiliating and sadistic mental punishment on David, tying a placard to him that reads *Take care of him. He bites.* This is what David's feelings are on this subject: "What I suffered from that subject, nobody can imagine" (130). He feels that he is under the pitilessly enquiring gaze of everyone as he walks around with his terrible burden.

What young children need is care and sympathy. In the educational premises of Creakle and the even more brutal and obnoxious Squeers in *Nicholas Nickleby* (1839) what they get is humiliation and chastisement in the name of education. What roused the indignation of Dickens and others like him is that this savage charade in the name of education was widely prevalent in England. Of course, physical punishment was meted out in the best and wealthiest of establishments. Even the much-venerated, reform-minded Dr Arnold resorted to it on occasion. However, in those cases the purpose was to form character and to instil discipline. Further, it was not punishment all the way; schoolboys had many recreational activities and rewards which meant that they exited the system with positive and sustaining memories.

No such extenuating circumstance attends the educational enterprises of Creakle and Squeers. One of the reasons why educational reformers such as James Kay Shuttleworth thought about teacher training colleges was that the wrong kind of people seemed to be becoming teachers, or worse still, teacher-proprietors. We are informed that Creakle "had been, a good many years ago, a small hopdealer in the Borough, and had taken to the school business after being bankrupt in hops, and making away with Mrs Creakle's money" (138). In the Preface to *Nicholas Nickleby* Dickens points out, in stinging words, how lack of ability and proper training combined had created educational anarchy:

> Of the monstrous neglect of education in England, and the disregard of it by the State as a means of forming good or bad citizens and miserable or happy men, private school long afforded a notable example. Although any man who had proved his unfitness for any other occupation in life, was free, without examination or qualification, to open a school anywhere . . . and although schoolmasters as a race, were the blockheads and impostors who might naturally be expected to spring from such a state of things, and to flourish in it; these Yorkshire schoolmasters were the lowest and most rotten round in the whole ladder. (Author's Preface xiv)

Dickens does note an improvement in the state of affairs at the time of writing *Nicholas Nickleby*. However, towards the end of his career he didn't seem to be holding positive views about education and educators. In his penultimate completed novel *Great Expectations*, "education" is reduced to the attainment of trivial accomplishments and elegant manners. Also, at a certain early moment in the narrative, we see that local education is just a joke where children make merry while a sleepy old woman nods away. In his last completed novel *Our Mutual Friend* (1865), we have the disturbing portrait of Bradley Headstone, who, as his last name suggests, is associated with death rather than life-giving education.

Many of the teaching malpractices took place in remote places safely away from the possibility of investigation and intervention. Arthur A. Adrian points out that the little village of Bowes which had twenty schools like Dotheboys Hall, flourished in its pernicious abuse of education because of the remoteness: "Being an out-of-the-way place, nearly three hundred miles from London, and at least two days' journey by coach, such a hamlet as Bowes was ideal for this traffic in unhappy schoolboys. Unable to reach home of their own accord, the pupils could not keep their parents informed of actual conditions" (238). While the problem with these schools was both lack of basic competence as well as lack of basic humanity on the part of the educators, the problem of incompetence was not confined to these privately run secluded schools. As Adrian says, "In the national schools, for example, teachers whose background was anything but academic were often employed. Usually the men who undertook the instruction of the young could succeed at nothing else. Even parish clerks and chapel cleaners, once they were incapacitated for regular service, entered the teaching profession" (238–39).

While we mainly remember the viciousness or sheer vocational unfitness of teachers or educators such as Creakle, Squeers, Gradgrind and Bradley Headstone in Dickens, we do come across a few sympathetic portraits as well. There is the kindly schoolteacher who helps little Nell and her grandfather in *The Old Curiosity Shop*, and the subdued Mell in *David Copperfield* as compensatory representations. Elsewhere in Victorian literature we find portraits of decent, humane schoolteachers quietly doing their jobs, imparting private tuition to needy students. Such, for example, is the man Bartle Massey in *Adam Bede*, who sets aside his rough nature as he affectionately teaches the honestly toiling poor workmen under his tutelage.

Poverty certainly darkened the educational scene in Victorian England, affecting educator and educated alike. The poor parish schoolmaster described in *Sketches by Boz* (published in book form in 1836), humble and fairly conscientious in the discharge of his duties but meeting with no earthly rewards, is a reasonably accurate representative. He is a lot like Mell in *David Copperfield*, the lower-class teacher who has a mother in the poorhouse and who is mocked by the students, most viciously by the upper-class Steerforth, for his low status. The examples of the teachers in college are also pertinent in highlighting the poverty equations prevalent in the educational spheres: poor teachers hoping to move up in life by teaching *poor* children from the workhouses. Their very failures are symbolic of the struggles of numerous students and teachers in a society that sets great store by the graph of ambition and progress. The sufferings of the tormented children in *Nicholas Nickleby* and to a lesser extent in Lowood School in *Jane Eyre* can be traced to the fact that their parents do not have the incomes to send them to warm, comfortable institutions that would be homes away from home. However, all these children still had education, however shabbily and roughly such education was imparted. It could be argued that it seems better not to have education than to be the recipients of the kind of education that is imparted as regular fare in Dotheboys Hall – but then there might be some fictional exaggeration in this. Many children in the Victorian age had to actually go without education. One such is the working-class child in *Sybil* who lives in such darkness of ignorance that she confuses Jesus Christ with Pontius Pilate. While the light of education often did not fall on the neglected children of industrialised towns such as Liverpool, Bradford and Manchester, the situation of the street children of London was also not very good. It was for the benefit of such children that the concept of the ragged school was formulated. The ragged school system was devised to provide education to the very poor in industrial cities as well as in London. The Ragged School Union formed in 1844 sought to extend the benefits of education by also providing food and clothing etc. Reading, writing, arithmetic and the Bible were normally taught.

Dickens supported this system although he had reservations about it not being secular, with words that also provided a kind of definitional justification: "They who are too ragged, wretched, filthy, and forlorn, to enter any other place: who could gain admission into no charity school, and who would be driven from any church door; are invited to come here" ("Crime"). In this essay entitled "Crime and Education," Dickens anticipates modern welfare theorists and thinkers who make the case that it is to society's advantage to clothe, shelter, feed and *educate* its poor, lest they become malcontents and turn against society.

The Education Act of 1870 tried to carry out the principles of the 1867 Reform Act with its vision of a nation-wide and free education for all children. It was drafted by the reformer W. E. Forster who was responding to the demands of political parties as well as different religious denominations. The Act tried to restore order and homogeneity by introducing National Schools. For this purpose, school districts and school boards were created. For a long part of the century both school and college education was under the tutelage of the Church authorities. Affiliation to the Anglican Church was important in the matter of both admission and employment, particularly in the universities. As for school education, the Church had their own "national schools" which were opened in the first decades of the nineteenth century. The Education Act of 1870 and various other measures eroded the Church's authority in religious education.

Before thc 1870 Act also there were reformative moves. In 1858 it was recommended by a commission that local education boards be set up to make education more orderly and meaningful. The 1867 Reform Act had as one of its aims compulsory and free education for children in the age group of five to thirteen years. The 1870 Act tried to fulfil these ambitions. The country was divided into 2568 school districts and the same number of locally-elected school boards were set up (These boards would, however, be abolished through the Education Bill of 1902.) with the following areas of jurisdiction: identifying places for schools and creating new schools if necessary; the enforcement of compulsory attendance; and remission of fees for poor students. It would take a while for these measures to attain complete success, especially in the matter of providing free and compulsory education for all.

These reforms, envisaging a greater role for the State and with a thrust towards democratisation, would also encounter opposition from diverse quarters. There was resistance from the Church which did not want their monopoly to be encroached upon by secular forces. Some feared that education would become a means for social control. Some others felt that the idea of mass or universal education would be a synonym for a flattening mediocrity. It was also felt that the working classes, whom the reformers wanted to be educated so that they became enlightened voters and citizens, might become too demanding and militant. However, a glance at works written by the likes of Dickens, Gaskell and Kingsley justifies the acute necessity of bringing the poor within the scope of education and also to provide education that was more humane and purposeful. Educational reforms for the masses were thus desirable and unstoppable.

It is not as if, however, that all the soul-searching and anguish in the matter was reserved for the children of poor families. Many of the educational projects, at government and private initiatives, tried to address the problem of middle and upper-class children. There was discontent regarding many aspects of education. The classical curriculum was one particular sore point and target of scrutiny and criticism.

This classical curriculum, criticised by writers as diverse as Thomas Hughes and Samuel Butler, with its valorisation of the "dead" languages, Latin and Greek, was found to be inadequate for the needs of the modern world. In the early and mid-Victorian periods, science had made some headway and had made enough difference to the lives of the people for it to be felt that subjects like the physical sciences and other related subjects with practical relevance deserved a more prominent place than Latin and Greek with their quaint and dated lessons. The thrust for a more appropriate and enabling educational system took place in the context of widespread reforms in all areas – religion, politics, women's rights. The reformist spirit functioned with the liberal understanding that different aspects of life were intermeshed, and reform in one sector necessitated reform in other areas as isolated and piecemeal reform would be exercises in futility. The Whigs/Liberals were the dominant forces in Victorian England, and unlike the Tory conservatives who stuck to past tradition, wanted to forge ahead with reformist agendas of progress and revision.

Another dominant force at this time was the middle-class. The middle-class included some of the rural gentry as well as some of the new urban professional classes who could afford quality education. While the poor went without education in many cases or were grateful for what smattering of education they could pick up, the middle and upper classes wanted an education that would help their wards get on in the world. "Getting on" (an expression that was much in vogue in this ambitious age and criticised by writers such as Carlyle, Kingsley and Ruskin) would include, among other things, landing coveted posts in the army and the colonial bureaucracy.

The mindlessness of the old system of learning, with the mandated emphasis on the classical languages of antiquity (Latin, Greek and even Hebrew) is exposed to satire by Charles Dickens in *Dombey and Son* (through the portrayal of Dr Blimber's Academy) and by Samuel Butler in the autobiographical *The Way of All Flesh*. This latter book explodes many Victorian pieties and myths, including those pertaining to family bonhomie, religious salvation, and education at home and in the institutions. The sorely oppressed Ernest Pontifex's teaching commences at home with theological notions drilled into him through regular beatings. The exaggerated and feverish religiosity of the mother Christina is captured in these lines: "The Jordan had left its bed and flowed into her own house" (104; Ch. 21) . A few lines after this we read: "When Ernest was in his second year, Theobald (his father) began to teach him to read. He began to whip him two days after he had begun to teach him" (105).

Butler emphasises that Ernest and presumably others like him grow up sickly and spiritless under a harsh and claustrophobic familial and educational regimen: "This was how it came to pass that their children were white and puny; they were suffering from *home-sickness.* They were starving, through being over-crammed with the wrong things" (125). And what are some of these "wrong things"? Latin and Greek, for instance: "Enough that he struggled through them (his earlier years) and at twelve years old knew every page of his Latin and Greek grammars by heart" (125). As Butler describes the further course of his life, it is patent that this learning stands the boy in no good stead. If he still turns out to be good and worth caring for, it is because of his innate spirit and liveliness which the parents and the schoolmasters fail to crush out of him after all. While his explorations of life (his sexual adventures, for example) frequently land him in trouble, he finally turns out all right, no thanks to the Latin and Greek and the religious catechism to which he is subjected.

In the evergreen boy's tale, *Tom Brown's School Days* (1857), Thomas Hughes seems to make a similar plea for good, hearty, animal spirits to prevail at the cost of a classically-oriented curriculum, through the thoughts of the protagonist's father: "Shall I tell him to mind his work, and say he's sent to school to make himself a good scholar? Well, but he isn't sent to school for that – at any rate, not for that mainly. I don't care a straw for Greek particles, or the digamma; no more does his mother . . . If he'll only turn out a brave, helpful, truth-telling Englishman, and a gentleman, and a Christian, that's all I want"(61; Ch. 4). In the matter of resisting rigorous and anachronistic classical education, there seems to be a convergence of viewpoints between Butler and Hughes. However, there are differences as well which need to be considered when we analyse the slant of reform in Victorian England. Butler savages religious education while Hughes is not averse to it, as the quote makes clear. Also, Butler satirises public school headmasters such as Dr Skinner and others, while the most important figure in Hughes's novel, apart from Tom Brown, is Dr Arnold, the great headmaster of Rugby School.

When we appraise the career of Dr Arnold, we appreciate that, like so many other things, reform of education was no simple and linear affair. Dr Arnold was credited with changing the course of school education, and he and his Rugby School are almost synonymous with the finest that the public school system could deliver. Dr Arnold entered the scene when education even for the reasonably affluent classes was in poor shape. Lytton Strachey captures the scenario in memorable language:

> The public schools of those days were still virgin forests, untouched by the hand of reform . . . It was a system of anarchy tempered by despotism. Hundreds of boys, herded together in miscellaneous boarding-houses, or in that grim 'Long Chamber' at whose name in after years aged statesmen and warriors would turn pale, lived, badgered and overawed by the furious incursions of an irascible little old man carrying a bundle of birch-twigs, a life in which licensed barbarism was mingled with the daily and hourly studies of the niceties of Ovidian verse. (128)

With zeal and intelligence, Dr Arnold cleaned up the system to a large extent, earning general admiration from the public, and veneration from the often unruly boys. We see the spirit of veneration shining in many pages of *Tom Brown's School Days,* the best known of the literary works on public school education: "What was it that moved and held us, the rest of the three hundred reckless, childish boys, who feared the Doctor with all our hearts, and very little besides in heaven or earth . . . we listened . . . to a man whom we felt to be, with all his heart and soul and strength, striving against whatever was mean and unmanly and unrighteous in our little world" (118; Ch. 7).

Arnold, who appears simply as the doctor for the better part of the narrative is no traditional, narrow-minded moralist. He advocates the health of life and limb and encourages the boys to play games such as football and cricket. He also tinkers a bit with curriculum by introducing subjects such as modern history, modern languages, and mathematics. By the standards of his times, he was a progressive and a reformer. But he did not drastically change things. He retained classical studies and also tried to inculcate Christian ethics into the souls of the boys. Although science was making its presence felt when Dr Arnold took over the headmastership of Rugby School in 1827, and was even more of a factor in changing perceptions of life when he died, Arnold and other headmasters of the great public schools such as Eton, Harrow, and Shrewsbury remained old-fashioned in many ways. They all clung to the classics and religious instruction. Science often had to develop in other ways than through systematic training in schools and colleges. As we have seen, the scientists of the day often had to work independently, undertaking expeditions near home and in far lands, educating themselves.

The concept of "muscular Christianity" is associated with Dr Arnold. The boys are not only exhorted to play physical games, but their tendency to frequently fight among themselves is also connived at. Actually the word "manly" recurs and resonates in Victorian literature, carrying a double meaning of physical valour and moral uprightness. Hughes quite explicitly endorses the value of fighting: "It is no good for Quakers, or any other body of men, to uplift their voices against fighting. Human nature is too strong for them, and they don't follow their own precepts. Every soul of them is doing his own piece of fighting, somehow and somewhere" (232; Ch. 5). Other authors also seemed to believe that the best side of human character often comes out in fighting situations, as when we see the awkward, unprepossessing Dobbin stepping into the defence of the small

George Osborne bullied by a bigger boy in Thackeray's *Vanity Fair.* After the contest is over and Dobbin comes out on top, he earns appreciation from all, although the acutely class-perceptive Thackeray shows George Osborne as actually being somewhat ashamed of his champion. This reminds us that apart from being centres and destinations of pedagogical excellence, and seats of moral training, the public schools were also sites where class-consciousness or class-superiority was learned or affirmed.

But like so many other instances of social mobility in Victorian culture, the public schools also provide the means to upgrade one's status. Dobbin becomes a major in the army, which was a prestigious post. Harry East, a fun-loving and mischievous character in Hughes's novel, who incarnates the ethos of manliness as much as anybody else through his fondness for scrapping, also joins the colonial army. With all its moral aims and Christian values, the public schools turned out to be crucibles where a certain kind of Englishman was produced – someone who would go into far lands brandishing the sword of the conqueror.

The hierarchic violence of the public school – older boys picking on "fags," bullying them, making them run errands, would also resurface in those distant lands in transmuted forms. Indeed, the rough-and-tumble (which sometimes had serious results, as the brother of the reformer Earl of Shaftsbury was killed in a school brawl) of the public schools was tolerantly regarded as a preparation for the sterner tests of life.

These public schools, with the involvement of the students in various escapades involving brushes with the authorities, clashes with property-owners who happened to be of the neighbourhood, and fights that very often ended with the appreciation of the opponents' pluck and spirit, forged enduring bonds. It could be argued that the success of British colonial enterprises or commercial and military ventures abroad was to a large extent owing to the camaraderie engendered in the playing-fields, as well as the dorms and class-rooms of the public schools. It is a truism to say that the battle of Waterloo, as well as the empire in general, was won in the playing fields of Eton.

In Rugby, it was Arnold himself who encouraged the older boys to take the younger boys under their wings, to create a certain hierarchy of loyalty and discipline that would last and prevail through rough times. However, so strong was the bond (often manifest in various forms of writing in school magazines) that it rose even above reverence for the teachers and Arnold himself. As William N. Weaver points out,

> By contrast with Arnold, however, Rugby schoolboy writings foreground peer identification more than identification with masters and attribute to the former many of the socializing and moralizing functions that Arnold attached to the latter. This celebration of school friendships as permanent male/male bonds modified Arnold's account of such friendships as necessarily characteristic of an immature age of development, thus reshaping the curve of his notion of schoolboy development. (458)

It also seems that in the writings there was some emulation of Romantic writers such as Shelley and Wordsworth, which is interesting, considering that childhood as a stage for strong influences working on the evolving personality is central to Romantic thought.

There is another fraught and contested area in the world of Victorian education and this is women's education, an area of neglect and darkness. Education for women was thought of in very limited terms. Much more than in the case of boys, a lot of "education" for girls was to be imparted at home. Even when more formal education was given to girls in seminaries and academies, what they were taught were petty, trivial accomplishments that certainly did not prepare the girls for the challenges of life or boost their self-esteem. They did not get the education to get jobs or to be able to stand on their own two feet. A typically condescending, patronising attitude created roadblocks for women in quest of better educational opportunities. On the one hand, it was felt that there were limits to what education could do for women, who were considered innately incapable of rising above a certain level. On the other, it was felt that the rigorous study of subjects and mathematics may damage their frail constitutions. A version of this view was that women might become "hardened" by education. (A similar fear was expressed regarding their employment.) As F. Knight points out, "To conservative Churchmen, the opening of higher education to women, which was beginning in a small way by 1870, spelled the creation of masculine women, who would reject their subordinate roles and become more domineering" (46). Not surprisingly, the Church was not too well-disposed towards female education.

Christopher Bischoff points out the "feminisation of education" which is however, misleading if taken out of context. All that he meant was that there would be more and more female teachers instead of male teachers as the century progressed. More *other* careers would open up for men while there would be correspondingly no increase in the opportunities available to women. In some ways education would be a circular kind of career. If women were the custodians of the right manners and pleasing but meaningless accomplishments such as dancing, sewing, drawing and music, they would perpetuate this powerless monopoly by teaching other girls who would go on to teach these same "accomplishments" to other girls or young women. The barrenness of this entire endeavour is well captured by Dickens in his portrayal of Mrs General in *Little Dorrit.*

Of course, feminists, educationists, and social activists would not allow the cycle to be perpetuated. The damaging idea about denying the girl-child her dues in education rested on the fostering of the myth that she would always have a shelter of home – first in the dwelling of her father and then in that of her husband. As already pointed out, many women would not have such a restful home after the deaths of their fathers because of dwindling marriage prospects, divorce and other socio-economic factors such as dislocations due to urbanisation. The situation was changing: marriage was not always an option, since many men and women were deliberately staying away from marriage. A diversifying world was also throwing open more career and employment opportunities. It was unjust to deny women the benefits of education under these changed circumstances. Harriet Martineau makes her claim in both practical terms and in the name of abstract principles:

> What we have to think of is the necessity, – in all justice, in all honour, in all humanity, in all prudence, – that every girl's faculties should be made the most of, as carefully as boys'. While so many women are no longer sheltered, and protected, and supported, in safety from the world (as people used to say) every woman ought to be fitted to take care of herself. Every woman ought to have that justice done to her faculties that she may possess in herself in all the strength and clearness of an exercised and enlightened mind, and may have at command, *for her subsistence* [emphasis mine], as much intellectual power and as many resources as education can furnish her with. (Ch. XXI)

There can be no longer clearer exposition and defence of women's needs in a time of change when the old securities and comforts were vanishing with the loosening of familial ties and social bonds.

The educationist Emily Davis, author of *The Higher Education of Women* (1866), fought hard for both secondary and higher education for women and achieved certain notable successes such as securing the admissions of girls to the Local Examinations of Cambridge University. She, along with Lady

Stanley of Alderly and Barbara Bodichon, opened the Girton College for Women in 1869. Among men, John Stuart Mill was one of the few who echoed views such as those espoused by Martineau and came out strongly in support of women's needs in the matter: "The claim of women to be educated as solidly, and in the same branches of knowledge, as men, is urged with growing intensity, and with a great prospect of success; while the demand for their admission into professions and occupations hitherto closed against them, becomes every year more urgent" (484–85). Among men of religion, clergyman Benjamin Parsons, a Congregationalist minister, was one of the few to support women's education, although he still had his eyes on the requirements of domesticity. There were quite a few boarding schools for girls, such as the ones to which the Brontës and George Eliot went.

The very brilliance and success against all odds of the women writers (among novelists George Eliot, the Brontë sisters, Elizabeth Gaskell, and among poets, Elizabeth Barrett Browning, and Christina Rossetti, to name the best known) underscore the unjust, asymmetrical educational set-up in Victorian times. Women like George Eliot (her real name was Marian Evans), not quite having the benefits of full and extended education like her male counterparts, still impressed everyone with her intellectual accomplishments and sheer learning. In her autobiographical novel, *The Mill on the Floss*, she shows the unfairness of family and society in becoming preoccupied with the education of a boy while neglecting the girl. Maggie Tulliver is a bright, clever girl, with a great aptitude for reading and learning things quickly. Her doting father acknowledges this, but still holds on to retrograde views about women's ambitions: "She understands what one's talking about so as never was. And you shall hear her read – straight off, as if she knowed it all beforehand. And allays at her book! But it's bad – it's bad . . . a woman's no business wi' being so clever; it'll turn to trouble, I doubt" (17; Bk 1, Ch. 3).

As for Tom, this is what the father has to say: "Well, he isn't not to say stupid – he's got a notion o' things out o' door, an' a sort o' common sense, as he'd lay hold o' things by the right handle. But he's slow with his tongue, you see, and he reads but poorly, and can't abide the books, and spells all wrong, they tell me . . ." (20).

Yet, in the early part of the narrative Tulliver and his relations and friends all worry about where Tom is going to study after his stint at a privately-run small academy. On the other hand, except for a stray thought that passes through the mind of Mrs Pullett, – a mere "half-formed notion", people are not bothered with Maggie's education. This is not some kind of individual fault or prejudice on the part of anyone, but general cultural bias. Interestingly the father, despite his lack of grammatical skills reflective of poor education, is actually quite perceptive. He has a genuine appreciation of education, but his apprehension about a "clever" woman facing trouble also turns out to be correct in a way, as Maggie dies a tragic death at the end.

Not surprisingly, the subject of education preys on the minds of women writers who thematise it in different ways. The Brontës had a fascination for education in real life. As bad education at the school owned by Carus Wilson at Cowan Bridge claimed the lives of two of their sisters Maria and Elizabeth, it is not surprising that Charlotte Bronte makes education fairly central in works such as *The Professor*, *Jane Eyre* and *Villette*. Also, in their own lives they had different experiences involving education. Compelled to be teachers and governesses at different times to support the household and not enjoying those roles much, they pursued a dream of starting a school on their own all their brief lives. In the words of Phyllis Bentley, "(t)he young Brontës' contacts with the outer world always occurred in the sphere of education" (34). As students and teachers/governesses they periodically left home. Charlotte and Emily also went to Brussels to receive teacher training as such facilities were deemed superior in the Continent. Charlotte's novels, *The Professor* and *Villette,* reflect her Brussels experience. However, their dreams of an ideal school would never be fulfilled.

Education occasionally plays a part in the portrayal of man–woman relationships in Victorian narratives. This shows the wide applicability of education as a theme in the literary landscape and reflects the concern of Victorians with various aspects of education. In *Sylvia's Lovers*, Philip Hepburn tries to educate Sylvia in what is very much a labour of love. In one scene, he brings a copy-book with the picture of the Tower of London in it, and tries to make Sylvia fill it up with "as pretty writing as any in t'North Riding" (92, Ch. 8). However, Sylvia cannot reciprocate the romantic sentiment and she is "unenlivened by this prospect" and displays "determined dumbness" (92–93).

Sylvia does not have the emotional maturity at this stage to appreciate the honest, earnest Philip as a suitor, and so repulses his attempts to educate her, although her own mother is very much for it. Gaskell quietly and unobtrusively seems to be making a plea for female education here. The flighty Sylvia, refusing wholesome if dull education at this point, will actually express a desire for some education later, when she is chastened by suffering. She pays the price for early frivolity and insensitivity in refusing Philip's help, losing almost everything at the end, being harshly "educated" by life. In *Shirley*, we have something like a reversal of the situation in *Sylvia's Lovers*. In one scene, Caroline Helstone mentally resists the education given by Hortense, the teacher of French, but learns quickly and delightedly when the teacher is Robert Moore, the man she loves.

There is a reversal of a different kind in *Wuthering Heights*, also in the context of a man–woman relationship. Here it is a woman who teaches a man, in scenes of growing intimacy. The younger Catherine sows seeds of knowledge in Hareton's head, and thus steals into his heart. Hareton is brutalised by Heathcliff denying any education to him, but he is tamed by the civilising power of education. And the novel, after its numerous strifes and antagonisms draws to a harmonious close, emerging from a darkness of ignorance, resentment and violence in a manner that would please an educational visionary.

The highest institutes of learning such as Cambridge and Oxford were not very friendly towards women's educational aspirations. In the Victorian period it was only London University which gave women full membership, in the year 1878. Oxford and Cambridge accommodated women only in the twentieth century, Cambridge giving full membership as late as 1948! The nineteenth century saw the doorways of education gradually widen for women, as also for other disadvantaged groups such as religious minorities. The establishment of colleges such as Bedford and Girton are landmarks for women's education in England. However, decades of struggle lay ahead.

As one can see, education was as contested and controversial a subject as any. Reformers and educationists made headway in the matter of providing education to the children of the poor, religious minorities and women often in the face of stiff opposition from reactionary and conservative elements of society. Writers played their part too, coming up with stark scenarios of poorly provided education or absence of education.

Works Cited

Adrian, Arthur A. " 'Nicholas Nickleby' and Educational Reform." *Nineteenth Century Fiction* 4.3 (Dec. 1949): 237–41. Web. 20 July 2015.

Bentley, Phyllis. *The Brontës.* London: Thames and Hudson, 1997. Print.

Bischoff, Christopher. "Masculinity, Social Mobility, and the Plan to End Pauperism in Mid-Victorian England: Kneller Hall Teacher's Training College." *Journal of Social History* 46.4 (Summer 2013): 1039–59. Published by Oxford UP. Project Muse. Web. 26 June 2015.

Butler, Samuel. *The Way of All Flesh*. London: Jonathan Cape, 1948. Print.

Dickens, Charles. *Nicholas Nickleby*. London: J. M. Dent, 1977. Print. Everyman's Library.

———. Author's Preface to *Nicholas Nickleby*. xiv–xviii.

———. *Hard Times*. Oxford: Oxford UP, 1989. Print. Oxford World's Classics.

———. *David Copperfield*. Harmondsworth, Middlesex, England: Penguin Books, 1966. Print. The Penguin English Library.

———. "Crime and Education." *Miscellaneous Papers: Essays from The Examiner, Household Words, and All the Year Round*. Web. 25 April 2015. < https://ebooks.adelaide.edu.au/d/dickens/charles/>.

Eliot, George. *The Mill on the Floss*. Oxford: Oxford UP, 1992. Print. World's Classics.

Gaskell, Elizabeth, *Sylvia's Lovers*. Oxford: Oxford UP, 2008. Print. World's Classics.

Hughes, Thomas. *Tom Brown's School Days*. London: Harper Press, 2013. Print. Collins Classics.

Knight, F. " 'Male and Female He Created Them': Men, Women and the Question of Gender." *Religion in Victorian Britain: Volume V Culture and Empire*. Ed. John Wolffe. Manchester: Manchester UP, 1997. 23–57. Print.

Martineau, Harriet. *Household Education*. Web. 22 May 2015. <https://archive.org/details/householdeducati00mart>.

Mill, John Stuart. "The Subjection of Women." *On Liberty and Other Essays*. Oxford: Oxford UP, 1991. 471–582. Print. The World's Classics.

Schlicke, Paul. "Introduction." *Hard Times*. vii–xxiii.

Strachey, Lytton. "Dr Arnold." *Eminent Victorians*. Radford VA: Wilder Publications, 2008. 126–47. Print.

Weaver, William N. " 'A School-Boy's Story': Writing the Victorian Public Schoolboy Subject." *Victorian Studies* 46.3 (Spring 2004): 455–87. Project Muse. Web. 25 May 2015. <http://muse.jhu.edu/article/173488>.

Webb, Igor. *From Custom to Capital: The English Novel and the Industrial Revolution*. Ithaca and London: Cornell UP, 1981. Print.

Timeline

Events	Important Publications
1829: Catholic Emancipation Act, facilitates entry of Catholics to Parliament and to some civil offices	
1830: Liverpool to Manchester railway line inaugurated, first to depend entirely on steam power	William Cobbett, *Rural Rides*
1832: First Reform Act ushers in parliamentary reforms	Charles Lyell, *Principles of Geology*
1833: Abolition of slavery in all British colonies through the Slavery Abolition Act; Factory Act prohibits the employment of children under 9; The Oxford Movement begins	
1834: Poor Law Amendment, also known as the New Poor Law; workhouses for the poor set up	Thomas Carlyle, *Sartor Resartus*
1836: Beginning of Chartism	Charles Dickens, *Pickwick Papers*
1837: Queen Victoria ascends to the throne of England	Thomas Carlyle, *The French Revolution*

1838: Anti-Corn Law League; People's Charter for universal suffrage	Dickens, *Oliver Twist;* Wordsworth, *Sonnets*
1839: Chartist Riots; Jamaica constitutional crisis: revolt of plantation owners	Dickens, *Nicholas Nickleby*; Charles Darwin, *The Voyage of the Beagle*
1840: Queen Victoria marries Prince Albert	Dickens, *The Old Curiosity Shop*
1842: Edwin Chadwick Report on the sanitary conditions of the Working Classes	Dickens, *Martin Chuzzlewit*; Browning, *Dramatic Lyrics*
1844: Factory Act restricts working hours of women and children. Third Reform Bill grants agricultural workers the right to vote	Disraeli, *Coningsby;* Robert Chambers, *The Vestiges of Creation*
1845–1849: Potato Famine in Ireland	Frederick Engels, *Condition of the Working Class in England;* Disraeli, *Sybil*
1846: Corn Laws repealed, import of foreign grains permitted	
1847:	Charlotte Bronte, *Jane Eyre;* Emily Bronte, *Wuthering Heights*

1848: Public Health Act following cholera outbreak in London; End of Chartist movement; Revolution breaks out in many parts of Europe	Marx and Engels, *Communist Manifesto;* Anne Bronte, *The Tenant of Wildfell Hall*; Elizabeth Gaskell, *Mary Barton*; Thackeray, *Vanity Fair;* J. S. Mill, *Principles of Political Economy;* Dickens, *Dombey and Son*
1849:	Charlotte Bronte, *Shirley;* Macaulay, *History of England;* Arthur Hugh Clough, *Amours de Voyage*
1850:	Alfred Lord Tennyson, *In Memoriam*; Thackeray, *The History of Pendennis*; Dickens, *David Copperfield;* Charles Kingsley, *Alton Locke*
1851: Great Exhibition in the Crystal Palace, Hyde Park. Gold discovered in Australia	Henry Mayhew, *London Labour and the London Poor*; John Ruskin, *The Stones of Venice*
1852: David Livingston's trans-African journey	Dickens, *Bleak House*; Thackeray, *Henry Esmond*
1853:	Arnold, *Poems*; Charlotte Bronte, *Villette*; Gaskell, *Ruth, Cranford*
1854: Siege of Sebastopol in Anglo-Russian Crimean War	Coventry Patmore begins *The Angel in the House* (completes in 1962); Dickens, *Hard Times*
1855:	Gaskell, *North and South*

1857: Establishment of Divorce Courts; Beginning of Indian War of Independence	Dickens, *Little Dorrit,* gives readings of *A Christmas Carol*; Charlotte Bronte, *The Professor*; Elizabeth Barrett Browning, *Aurora Leigh*; Anthony Trollope, *Barchester Towers*; Thomas Hughes, *Tom Brown's School Days*
1858: End of Indian War following which powers of East India Co. transferred to the Crown	George Eliot, *Scenes of Clerical Life*
1859:	Charles Darwin, *Origin of Species*; Eliot, *Adam Bede*; Samuel Smiles, *Self-Help*; Tennyson, *Idylls of the King*; Dickens, *A Tale of Two Cities*
1860:	Eliot, *The Mill on the Floss*
1861: Prince Albert dies	Dickens, *Great Expectations*; Eliot, *Silas Marner*
1862: Famine among Lancashire cotton workers	Meredith, *Modern Love*; Christina Rossetti, *Goblin Market and Other Poems*; Charles Kingsley, *The Water Babies*
1864: Karl Marx organises First Socialist International in London	Newman, *Apologia pro Vita Sua*

1865: William Booth founds Salvation Army	Mathew Arnold, *Essays in Criticism*; Lewis Carroll, *Alice's Adventures in Wonderland*
1866:	Eliot, *Felix Holt*; Swinburne, *Poems and Ballads*
1867: Second Reform Act, electorate doubled	Marx, *Das Kapital*; Trollope, *The Last Chronicle of Barset*
1868: Trades Union Congress founded	
1869: Girton College for women established	Arnold, *Culture and Anarchy*; Browning, *The Ring and the Book*; J. S. Mill, *On the Subjection of Women*
1870: The First Married Women's Property Act, women get right to retain money they earn; National School system instituted through Education Act	
1871: Abolition of religion tests (meant to determine eligibility for admission to universities)	Darwin, *The Descent of Man*; Eliot, *Middlemarch*; Trollope, *The Eustace Diamonds*
1873: Beginning of agricultural depression	Walter Paper, *Studies in the History of the Renaissance*
1874:	Thomas Hardy, *Far from the Madding Crowd*

1876: Victoria declared empress of India	Eliot, *Daniel Deronda*
1878:	Hardy, *The Return of the Native*
1879: Disraeli refuses protective tariffs for British farmers	
1881:	Henry James, *Portrait of a Lady*
1882: The Second Married Women's Property Act gives women the right to separate ownership of property	
1884: The Third Reform Bill: agricultural workers get right to vote	
1886:	Hardy, *The Mayor of Casterbridge*; Robert Louis Stevenson, *Dr Jekyll and Mr Hyde*
1887: 'Bloody Sunday' demonstrations in Trafalgar Square	Hardy, *The Woodlanders*
1889: London Dock strike	
1891:	Hardy, *Tess of the D'Urbervilles*; Oscar Wilde, *The Picture of Dorian Gray*
1893: Independent Labour Party formed	Gissing, *The Odd Women*

1894:	George Bernard Shaw, *Arms and the Man*
1895:	Hardy, *Jude the Obscure*
1897: Women's suffrage movement gains momentum	
1899: Boer War begins, opinion in England split	Joseph Conrad, *Heart of Darkness*
1901: Queen Victoria dies	
1903:	Samuel Butler, *The Way of All Flesh*

Index

Literary/Cultural Theory provides concise and lucid introductions to a range of key concepts and theorists in contemporary literary and cultural theory. Original and contemporary in presentation, and eschewing jargon, each book in the series presents students of humanities and social sciences exhaustive overviews of theories and theorists, while also introducing them to the mechanics of reading literary/cultural texts using critical tools.

Series Editors

Allen Hibbard, Middle Tennessee State University
Andrew Slade, University of Dayton
Herman Rapaport, Wake Forest University
Imre Szeman, University of Alberta
Krishna Sen, University of Calcutta
Scott Slovic, University of Idaho
Sumit Chakrabarti, Presidency University, Kolkata

Titles in the series

Feminisms
Psychoanalytic Theory and Criticism
Marxism
Postcolonialism
Poststructuralism and Deconstruction
New Historicism
New Criticism
Ecocriticism
Masculinities
Jacques Lacan

CRITICAL EDITIONS

Co-published by

The English and Foreign Languages University, Hyderabad

Orient BlackSwan

Series Editors

T. Sriraman, Lakshmi Chandra and Lavanya Kolluri
EFL-U, Hyderabad

About the series: *Critical Editions* is a series jointly published by the English and Foreign Languages University and Orient BlackSwan with the aim of bringing literary texts closer to students of both undergraduate and postgraduate levels. Each edition not only explores the structure and texture of the text chosen but also places it in its literary and cultural context. These editions are introduced and edited by reputed academic experts and are supported by their experience of teaching and interacting with students over a number of years.

Published

English Poetry 1660–1780: An Anthology
Edited by Pramod K. Nayar, Department of English, University of Hyderabad

Robinson Crusoe *by* Daniel Defoe
Edited by Pramod K. Nayar, Department of English, University of Hyderabad

Emma *by* Jane Austen
Edited by Sunita Mishra, Centre for English Language Studies, University of Hyderabad

Wuthering Heights *by* Emily Brontë
Edited by Sunita Mishra, Centre for English Language Studies, University of Hyderabad

Gulliver's Travels *by* Jonathan Swift
Edited by Pramod K. Nayar, Department of English, University of Hyderabad

Modern English Poetry: A Selection
Edited by Mohan G. Ramanan, Department of English, University of Hyderabad

Tess of the d'Urbervilles *by* Thomas Hardy
Edited by John Varghese, The English and Foreign Languages University (EFL-U)

